language differences: do they interfere?

JAMES L. LAFFEY

Indiana University

and

ROGER SHUY

Georgetown University

Editors

eic+ira

1973

International Reading Association

Newark, Delaware 19711

Language Differences: Do They Interfere? is based on papers presented at a preconvention institute at the 1971 International Reading Association convention at Atlantic City. Cochairmen of the Institute, which was called "Language Development and Reading," were James L. Laffey and Roger Shuy.

BILLIE S. STRUNK
Publications Editor

BRUCE TONE
Director of Publications

Library of Congress Catalog Card Number: 73-85157
Third Printing, September 1977

CONTENTS

FOREWORD Language is the means, and perhaps the only means, by which man can build a valid construct and/or model of reality and existence. Language can be a filter of bias which permits him to see, hear, taste, and feel that which his sensory modalities permit him to perceive. Inappropriate language skills may, therefore, give man a myopic view of his environment.

Language and the culture of a people are inextricably bound together. It is through language that the culture of a generation is transmitted to succeeding generations. A group's culture generates the language, but on the other hand, the language has a controlling effect upon the culture. Man, therefore, can be at one time both the sum of and the emissary of his culture—his perception of and reaction to his environment.

The problems which plague the dedicated teacher never cease. In fact, as the environment in which we live becomes increasingly complex, these problems seem not only to increase but they appear to be compounded as the school years roll by. As each minority group assumes a nationalistic identity through its own efforts, those in the field of education, and especially in the language arts, suddenly become aware of new challenges— challenges which they must meet without bias or unsavory emotions.

The repertoire of language skills brought by the child to the classroom will give alert and efficient teachers a unique insight into their experiential background, mores, personalities, and educational needs. More important, the language skills of the dialectically different child can form a solid matrix upon which can be organized a viable reading/learning environment.

Language Differences: Do They Interfere? is a provocative title for this volume. The editors have assembled a group of papers that every teacher, whether teaching in rural America or in suburban or urban sections of our cities, should study carefully

NONSTANDARD DIALECT PROBLEMS:

An Overview

Roger W. Shuy
Georgetown University

It was six men of Indostan
To learning much inclined
Who went to see the Elephant
(Though all of them were blind)
That each by observation
Might satisfy his mind.

Thus begins John Godfrey Saxe's famous parable of the Blind Men and the Elephant, a poem which has been used to illustrate differing viewpoints, overgeneralizations, incomplete data, prejudice, and many other factors which interfere with complete understanding. Describing the elephant may have been about as difficult as providing an overview of the nonstandard dialect problem today. It might prove painful to try to extend this analogy further (for example, the phonics advocates might be characterized as seeing only the elephant's ear). But the principle of differing viewpoints most assuredly characterizes the state of the art today. In presenting an overview of the nonstandard dialect problem, we must assess the situation from as many perspectives as seem reasonable and in as many matrices as the problem really exists.

One set of viewpoints, for example, involves the viewer's role. Researchers, teachers, publishers, parents, community leaders, and the general public tend to see life differently, and it is no small problem to reconcile their drastically different viewpoints. A less global set of viewpoints may be those of the disciplines in which the research is being done. Researchers in linguistics, psychology, and reading also differ in their views of the problem. The third major matrix of viewpoints is that of the teaching strategies to be adopted. Some put pressure on the child to adapt to the school situation. Some put pressure on the teacher to adjust to the child. Some put pressure on the materials devel-

opers to build materials in such a way that neither the child nor
the teacher is put at a disadvantage.

Historically, the concern for the relationship of the child's
everyday language to his acquisition of reading is very recent.
It grew out of the concern of the schools for the child's oral
language (also very recent). Although it is true that linguists
have long argued for the importance of oral language to reading
(Bloomfield and Barnhart, 1961; Fries, 1963), it has been only
within the past decade that this concern has been interpreted
along the lines of different social dialects. And this is quite
natural since it has been only within the past decade that a
frontal attack has been mounted on the description of such
dialects. While such descriptions were being made, the national
mood for evaluation and accountability revealed that a large
number of those children who do poorly on standardized reading
tests are from minority homes—homes in which nonstandard
English is commonly used. Since it was argued by many linguists
and reading specialists that reading is a language processing
operation, it became clear that the potential effect of a child's
systematic spoken language on his reading ability should be
investigated. The calling of attention to this situation was her-
alded with, at best, mixed reactions. As early as 1964, Raven I.
McDavid, Jr. had urged reading specialists to pay attention to
children's language habits as they build materials and devise
methodologies. In 1965, Kenneth Goodman urged teachers to
accept their students' nonstandard oral renderings of the standard English page as acceptable reading. This position was
echoed by William Labov in 1966, when he suggested that one
task for the reading teacher is to learn the grammar of nonstandard English so that he will be able to better diagnose
reading problems. In 1968, Lloyd Leaverton and others designed
a reading program which was intended to avoid the problem of
introducing a different speech pattern at the same time the child
was learning to read. By 1969, when Joan Baratz and Roger
Shuy put forth a collection of articles which were intended to
call attention to this situation, one would think that the issue

might have been accepted for what it was—a highly interesting and important set of hypotheses which needed to be tested and either verified or rejected. But the issue of the potential mismatch of oral language and developing reading skills turned out to be considerably more passionate than anyone might have imagined.

The researcher's problem

Part of the problem stems from the newness of the issue. We are simply not prepared for the dimensions of the topic which recent developments have brought. For one thing, the social temper of our times is such that it is popular to be one-up on one's fellow researchers, not just academically but also attitudinally. That is, it has become popular to be able to imply, among other things, that someone else is racially prejudiced. To be sure, this may be manifestly true, but the game has led to considerable time wasting at serious discussions, and the search for new ways to be offended has led to little that is substantive in the issue. Such time wasting has often involved terminology (Fasold and Wolfram, 1970). Shall we use the terms *Negro, black, chicano, disadvantaged, inner-city,* or what? There is no satisfactory answer to the problem, and we might better be guided to assume good intentions on the part of the user, however naive he may be, and move to more substantive matters. Recently I witnessed a thirty-minute hassle over the term *subgroup,* which various minority participants felt was offensive. To have this objection poses no great problem (although Senate subcommittees might consider themselves equal to other senators or committees), but to impugn the motives of the user of the term is something which leads only to lengthy nonsubstantive arguments which can best be settled somewhere else. We could hope for something better.

Another aspect of the problem stems from the inevitable consequences of interdisciplinary activity. It is always difficult for psychologists, educators, linguists, and social scientists to work together since their beginning assumptions may be so divergent.

Words tend to be used differently by different disciplines, and priorities are bound to vary. Also, this particular issue in reading has challenged the very superstructure of the professional reading establishment. Many of the loudest voices are not "reading people" at all but are brash outsiders who must certainly threaten "things as they are."

In any case, it is hoped that by the time of this writing certain objections need no longer be made. It is highly questionable, for example, that any current researcher in this field is plying his wares because he feels that this is the best method of achieving racist goals. A dedicated racist would probably find greener pastures to work in. If this is true, the worst we can say of one another is that we are naive or stupid. I doubt that we are malicious.

By now it should be possible to refer to black children from low income, nonstandard English speaking homes without specifying all of this socioeconomic data on every mention that is made of them. It should also be clear that there are many reasons for the increased quantity of research done on black populations in the past few years. It has been popular in recent days for someone to stand up during a scholarly discussion and observe that it is a shame that all the research is being done on black children and none on white children. To this observation we must reply that, in both language and reading, practically all the research of the past fifty years in this country has been on white children. If the recent emphasis on black populations seems overbalanced, it must be seen against many years of benign (or malignant) neglect. In other words, the issues of our days should be substantive ones rather than matters of rhetoric.

The child's problem

The nonstandard dialect problem might best be seen in terms of the views of the child, the teacher, and the instructional system. That is, we might legitimately ask, "Who has the problem anyway?" Again, if we let history be our guide, we will see that the mismatch of the child's oral language to the printed page has been thought of largely as the child's problem by a majority of the researchers and teachers involved. There is a well-known stereotype in the educational world in which minority group children are said to be nonverbal, language-deficient, and culturally deprived. It has been my experience in the classrooms of such students that if I ask the teacher if she has a nonverbal child, she feels strangely obligated to nominate someone. Whether such a child actually exists or not, I have yet to be shown one who couldn't be turned-on verbally by the right stimuli and conditions.

What is apparently meant by the nonstandard dialect problem of the student is only that the child's speech does not correlate, one-to-one, with the expected speech patterns of the classroom. Several years ago, linguists began to try to determine exactly what this lack of exact correlation really meant. This is not the place to catalogue the research involved or to go into detail about it, but several important aspects of this research can be noted.

For one thing, nobody whose speech was studied intensively in certain northern ghetto communities produced the nonstandard form in all places and under all circumstances. If we listen long enough, if we talk about the right topics, and if we do not intimidate him, such a child will produce a stream of speech that much of the time is standard in its grammar and some of the time is stigmatized in its grammar and pronunciation. He may occasionally produce a vocabulary item that is related to street topics or some special jargon, but the listener will find that the aspects of his speech which are most stigmatized are grammar items.

The following aspects of grammar and phonology have been noted by Fasold and Wolfram (1970) as the major areas of stigmatization in the nonstandard speech used by urban northern blacks.

Pronunciation

1. Word final consonant clusters such as the /-st/ in *test* and *missed* or the /-nd/ in *find* or *canned.*
2. The /θ/ sounds in all positions as in *think, nothing,* and *tooth.*
3. /r/ and /l/ before consonants or at the end of words as in *help* and *sister.*
4. The devoicing or deletion of word final /b/, /d/, and /g/ as in *pig, salad,* and *tub.*
5. The collapse of /i/ and /e/ before nasal consonants, as in *pen/pin.*
6. Monophthongization of vowel glides as in *dime.*
7. Simplification of *a-an* distinctions as in *a egg.*
8. First syllable stress in words that otherwise have second syllable stress as in *hotel* and *police.*

Grammar

1. Nonactualized *-ed* inflection, as in *missed, started,* and *said.*
2. The presence of certain perfective construction as in *I done forgot* and *I been had it.*
3. No present tense verb third singular marker as in *He walk, He have a car,* and *He don't go.*
4. Future expressed as *He gonna go, I'ma go,* or *He see you tomorrow.*
5. The presence of a grammatical category, not found in standard English, called invariant *be* as in *Sometime he be busy.*
6. Nonactualized forms of the verb *to be* as in *He a good man.*
7. The use of *ain't* in the sense of *isn't* as well as *didn't* as in *He ain't here* and *He ain't do that,* respectively.
8. The extensive use of multiple negation as in *Nobody didn't know nothing.*

9. Nonactualized possessive markers as in *The boy coat,* and different possessive marker actualization as in *This he book* and *It mines.*

10. Nonactualized plural markers as in *five book,* and dual actualizations as in *two mens.*

11. The embedded question structure, *I want to know can he come out?*

12. The extensive use of pronomial apposition as in *My mother she went shopping.*

13. The use of existential *it,* as in *It's a lot of people out front.*

It must be noted, however, that most of the preceding features can be found also in the speech of many nonblacks who live in economically depressed areas. The differences between standard and nonstandard speech, then, are not always a matter of presence versus absence of a given feature. Instead, the difference is often a matter of frequency of occurrence. This may be a difficult concept to grasp, but it remains a fact that there is a distinct correlation between the frequency of occurrence of certain stigmatized grammatical and phonological features and socioeconomic status, style, age, race, and sex. Thus black children are said to use multiple negatives before indefinites (I don't have none), even though white children also produce such utterances. The phenomenon is stigmatized in the school environment in both cases, and the grammatical feature cannot be considered black English alone. The difference between its use by blacks and by whites of the same socioeconomic status is entirely quantitative. Both use multiple negatives, but research has pointed out that blacks use them more frequently.

One significant outgrowth of this situation which has yet to be answered involves the relationship of such linguistic variability to the kinds of evaluations which the schools make of children when the data upon which judgments are made are, at best, incomplete. What test situation could allow for variability? This is a question which deserves immediate attention.

The preceding distinction can be made of many of the grammatical and phonological characteristics of black English. Some characteristics, however, are almost categorically black. Included among them are the iterative *be*, "Most of the time he be here," but not the *be* which results from *will* or *would* reduction, "He be here tomorrow" and "He be here if he could," respectively, which can be found among many whites as well. Also on that list would be all three *-s* forms; noun plurals, verb third singular present tense, and possessive nouns. After the basic acquisition of the native language is completed, there are few documented cases of whites using these forms without *-s*.

Such a list as the one preceding, therefore, must be used with caution. Not all nonstandard speakers will use all of these forms. Not all such speakers will use them to the same extent or in the same context. These features do not represent pure black English or any kind of pure nonstandard speech. Instead they represent some of the things we now know about this highly complex area.

Research of this sort has led us one small step closer to an answer to the question of what it is that causes people's speech to be stigmatized. A great many things remain to be done. We know little about corresponding aspects of intonation and voice quality. We have only partial information about what happens during style shifting and code switching and relatively little information about the acquisition of social dialects during the early years of childhood and many other things.

The teacher's problem

Another way of looking at the nonstandard dialect problem is to see it from the view of the teacher. Perhaps he is the one who has the problem. Just as blame for communication breakdown cannot be placed entirely on the listener (the sender might well be at fault), so the language problems of the disadvantaged child cannot be viewed in isolation from the classroom.

Little research has been done on the effect of the speech of teachers as a model for child speech or on how the teacher is capable of creating negative views toward language, standard or not, in his students. In fact, relatively little research has been done on what the teacher knows, feels, or thinks about the language of disadvantaged pupils. Considerable data have been gathered on how a teacher is trained, on whether or not he feels adequately trained, and on what he actually does in the process of teaching, but assessments of what teachers really know about the language used by children and how they feel about it are infrequent. We know from *The National Interest and the Teaching of English* (1961) that the linguistic preparation of prospective English teachers is woefully inadequate. It should not be surprising, then, that teachers find it difficult to describe accurately the language problems of their disadvantaged students.

Teachers need to learn about the current research in urban language problems, why the research is being done, how it is carried out, what is known at the moment, and, every bit as important, what is not known. Further, teachers need to take cognizance of their own language in relation to that of their pupils. They need to understand language variation—the reasons underlying it and the attitudes of various subcultures toward it. Teachers should learn to listen to the language of their students. They should find out how systematic the language of disadvantaged children can be, and they should develop a sensitivity to the editing processes that take place as one person listens to another.

To accomplish this, the preparation of language arts teachers must be overhauled to put language at the center of the program, accompanied wherever possible by courses in administration, techniques, and evaluation. It is an indisputable fact that the most important tool for survival, for communicating, and for obtaining knowledge and skills is language. This is as true for middle-class children as for disadvantaged socioeconomic groups. But if the circumstances under which disadvantaged children acquire this tool militate in some way against their acquiring middle-class language patterns, some kind of special attention must be given to them. This special attention requires the teacher to develop an ability to learn how to deal with the child's language, how to listen and respond to it, how to diagnose what is needed, how best to teach alternate linguistic systems, and how to treat it as a positive and healthy entity. When viewed in this way, the nonstandard dialect problem must surely be seen as the teacher's problem.

The instructional system's problem

One might also view the nonstandard dialect problem as the problem of the instructional system. Having begun with a description of the differences between standard and nonstandard English and having addressed ourselves to some of the special needs of the teachers, we would be remiss to neglect the strategies and materials of the classroom.

Of the five current hypotheses concerning classroom strategies for dealing with the interrelationship of nonstandard dialect and reading, two focus on teacher training and perception (Kenneth Goodman's suggestion that teachers be taught to accept the dialect reading of materials written in standard English and the language experience method, which calls on the teacher's ability to accurately hear and record the child's own language); and the other three hypotheses focus heavily on the development or use of materials and/or special strategies of some sort.

One hypothesis is that children be taught standard English before they are taught to read. This requires no substantive change in reading materials, but it does require some special methods or materials which will help six-year-old children learn to speak standard English.

Linguists and anthropologists have generally been rather pessimistic about the possibility of teaching six-year-olds standard English because the peer-group influence over speech resists the attempts of classroom teachers to change speech patterns. The diversity of opinions concerning the amount of time and effort required to teach standard English to such children ranges anywhere from Venezky's estimate of a few months (1970) to Kochman's "never" (1969). Wolfram's assessment (1970) of the situation is:

> Before we can endorse teaching Standard English as a prerequisite for reading, we must have evidence that it can be extensively taught given the current sociocultural facts, and that it is most effectively taught at the initial stages of education. At this point, the sociocultural facts which inhibit the widespread acquisition of Standard English as a second dialect do not suggest this alternative as a reasonable solution.

Many people have reasoned that because it is good to learn standard English, it is good to learn it as soon as possible. What they have failed to take into consideration is the fact that we are grossly inefficient in teaching standard English at any level. Ralph Fasold (in press), in fact, seriously questions whether a second dialect can be taught at all. A second consideration (Kochman, 1969) is less of technology than of policy: should anyone be taught to speak standard English at all?

A second hypothesis has grown out of the work of Leaverton and Gladney and Baratz and Stewart, who argue that educators should practice what they have been preaching for years and start the reading process where the children are rather than forcing the children to adjust to the traditional materials. This approach would separate into two different tasks, the acts of learning standard English and learning to read. Most linguists who have considered the matter have agreed that the aspects of the text to be focused upon should be grammatical features, not phonology (Fasold, 1969; Shuy, 1969; Stewart, 1969). The very suggestion that black children might be grouped in some way has proved an offensive notion to many critics of dialect readers, but the major obstacle, no doubt, comes from the shock of seeing grammar that is not standard English actually in print without quotations and without the appearance of being narrative dialogue. A nation that feels uncomfortable with the dialect found in *Huckleberry Finn* may be expected to quiver when it is seen as a replacement for Dick and Jane. From this shock, it is a relatively simple matter to leap to unwarranted conclusions and

to one-up one's fellow educator by calling him racist or by otherwise impugning his motives. In the case of dialect readers, as
in all other hypotheses here, one might expect the success or
failure of the experimentation to outweigh subjective feelings—
but such has not proved to be the case.

The last hypothesis attempts to avoid the dangers of the dialect
readers and the uncharted waters of trying to teach children
standard English before they are taught to read. The "avoidance" or "neutralization" strategy would utilize material in which
the grammatical forms not used by a child in his speech are
avoided. This approach would not incorporate the child's nonstandard grammatical features but would exclude such potential
trouble spots as verb third singular -s forms, past tense, etc. for
a brief time early in the acquisition of reading, gradually introducing them at a later date in a slow and sequenced fashion. As
in the case of dialect readers, the pressure is placed on the
materials, not on the child (as in the case of the hypothesis which
suggests that children be taught standard English first), and
not on the teachers (as in the case of the hypotheses which
suggest that teachers accept dialect renderings of the standard
printed page or that they build their own materials using the
experience method).

The need for a total view

What, then, is the nonstandard dialect problem? Whose problem is it? Like the six men of Indostan who tried to describe
the elephant, psychologists, reading specialists, and linguists
today have attempted to describe the nonstandard dialect problem
from different perspectives. Perhaps, like those men, we have
each been partly in the right but also partly in the wrong in that
we have not viewed the problem in its entirety. There is no real
choice to be made between the child, the teacher, and the
instructional package. It is a problem for all three, depending
on any number of real or imagined circumstances. If the decision is made to teach a child to read and if it is determined that
language plays any role at all in the process, the situation must be
viewed from all three perspectives.

References

Baratz, Joan C., and Shuy, Roger W., Eds. *Teaching Black Children to Read.* (Washington, D.C.: Center for Applied Linguistics, 1969.)

Bloomfield, Leonard, and Barnhart, Clarence L. *Let's Read: A Linguistic Approach.* (Detroit: Wayne State University Press, 1961.)

Fasold, Ralph W. "Orthography in Reading Materials for Black English Speaking Children," *Teaching Black Children to Read,* Joan Baratz and Roger Shuy, Eds. (Washington, D.C.: Center for Applied Linguistics, 1969.)

Fasold, Ralph W. "What Can An English Teacher Do About Non-Standard Dialect?" *English to Speakers of Other Languages, Standard English to Speakers of Non-Standard Dialect,* Rodolfo Jacobson, Ed. Special anthology issue of *The English Record* (in press).

Fasold, Ralph W., and Wolfram, Walt. "Some Linguistic Features of Negro Dialect," *Teaching Standard English in the Inner City,* Ralph W. Fasold and Roger W. Shuy, Eds. (Washington, D.C.: Center for Applied Linguistics, 1970.)

Fries, Charles C. *Linguistics and Reading.* (New York: Holt, Rinehart and Winston, 1963.)

Goodman, Kenneth S. "Dialect Barriers to Reading Comprehension," *Elementary English,* 42 (December 1965), 853-60.

Kochman, Thomas. "Social Factors in the Consideration of Teaching Standard English," *Linguistic-Cultural Differences and American Education,* A. C. Aarons, et al., Eds. *Florida FL Reporter,* 7 (1969), 89.

Labov, William. "Some Sources of Reading Problems for Negro Speakers of Nonstandard English," *New Directions in Elementary English,* A. Frazier, Ed., 140-67. (Champaign, Illinois: National Council of Teachers of English, 1967.)

Leaverton, Lloyd, et al. *The Psycholinguistics Reading Series.* (Chicago Board of Education, 1969.)

McDavid, Raven I. "Dialectology and the Teaching of Reading," *Reading Teacher,* 18 (December 1964), 206-13.

Shuy, Roger W. "A Linguistic Background for Developing Beginning Reading Materials for Black Children," *Teaching Black Children to Read,* Joan Baratz and Roger Shuy, Eds. (Washington, D.C.: Center for Applied Linguistics, 1969.)

Squire, James R., et al. *The National Interest and the Teaching of Reading.* (Champaign, Illinois: National Council of Teachers of English, 1961.)

Stewart, William. "Negro Dialect in the Teaching of Reading," *Teaching Black Children to Read,* Joan Baratz and Roger Shuy, Eds. (Washington, D.C.: Center for Applied Linguistics, 1969.)

Venezky, Richard L. "Nonstandard Language and Reading," *Elementary English,* 47 (1970), 342.

Wolfram, Walt. "Sociolinguistic Alternatives in Teaching Reading to Nonstandard Speakers," *Reading Research Quarterly,* 6 (Fall 1970), 15-16.

COGNITION AND LANGUAGE:
Some Observations

NICHOLAS J. ANASTASIOW
Indiana University

My typical habit upon coming home from work in the evening is to read the newspaper. I first make a rapid change of clothes and then settle at the end of the kitchen table. Let me set the scene for you. Our kitchen is small; the refrigerator is near the table and comes on and off with a frequency that we are all used to, except, that is, on quiet nights when someone raises in bed and says "What's that?" My wife is also in the kitchen putting the last touches to dinner. And, about the time I'm ready to read the comics, my daughter comes in to set the table. There is occasional chit-chat, and the dog may eat the cat's food, or an unusual bird may light on the bird feeder outside the window. Throughout all of this, the radio is playing in the background. If I'm lucky, the local rock station has been switched to an FM station that plays popular music.

While I read the paper, I tune my wife and daughter in and out, watch a cardinal or two, and listen to the radio. Songs I selectively attend to are those that are my current favorites such as "Raindrops Keep Falling on My Head" and those I can't get away from such as "Theme from Love Story." Occasionally I'm aware of an old song that has been revived such as Peggy Lee's "Fever." The amount of distraction varies, but I am able to process both the written and the auditory stimuli.

Let us now change the stage. Our summer vacation was spent on Sanibel Island in Florida. My kitchen was transformed into a large motel efficiency apartment complete with air conditioning. Sanibel is off the southwestern tip of Florida, and the days and nights are warm and humid so the air conditioner was never turned off. The point is that I adjusted to the steady rhythm and

the changing tones as the thermostat accelerated or decelerated
the cooling process.

Since my ideal summer vacation is to swim, sun bathe, walk,
and read, I had a large supply of books to read each evening.
Now in this glorious scene the only element that distracted me
was the level of sound coming from our neighbors radio or TV.
I would occasionally remark that I wished they would turn down
the volume or change the station, but most of the time this was
a minor distraction. On our fourth day at Sanibel, it occurred
to me on my long morning walk that I was singing to myself
an amazing number of country-western songs. My wife is a
country music fan and consequently, through no fault of my
own, I can recognize a large number of country songs. However, as you might guess, it is not my typical pattern to sing
"Cold, Cold Heart." I remarked to my wife that the music was
getting to me, that I wished the motel neighbors would either
turn down their radio or TV or switch the station. My wife
remarked that it didn't bother her and, in general, she rarely
heard the music and doubted that it was TV but probably WSM,
the "Grand Ole Opry" station from Nashville, Tennessee. I
countered that it really sounded like our FM station at home
although they played a surprising amount of country music.

Before finishing the story, let me provide you with additional
background information. Prior to our vacation I had been reading
Gibson's work (1969) on perception and Norman's work (1969)
on attention. I was thinking a great deal about the relationship
of language and cognition and the role that selective attention
plays in thinking. Hence, the next events in my story:

Sanibel is a great shell beach and, as we were walking and
talking about the neighbor's music, we were also looking for
a particular type of shell. Suddenly, I was struck with how easy
it is to find a particular type of shell once you center your
attention to look for it. Drawing the analogy, I said to my wife,
"I know why you don't hear the music all the time as I do.
It's because there isn't any music, except occasionally when their
TV is on. Have you noticed that I hear the music in the motel

every time I read—in the morning as I read the newspaper as well as in the afternoon or evening when I read books?"

Now at this point I'm sure my wife saw me as if I were the Thurber husband who reported he had just seen the unicorn in the garden. However, she recognized, as in the Thurber story, there are dangers in suggesting that your husband is "mad" and encouraged me to explain.

What was occurring, I explained, was that I was reconstructing music from the noise frequency and rhythmic patterns made by the air conditioner. My habit was such that I had been "set" to listen for music through the maze of kitchen noises of wife, daughter, stove, and, particularly, the refrigerator. In the motel I "found" music in the patterns presented by the air conditioner. Upon returning from the walk, I listened to the air conditioner and discovered it had three set patterns: a high-rapid acceleration, a steady-medium flow, and a lower rate. These patterns were repeated, and within each I had constructed musical patterns resembling the repetitious patterns of country music. To put it another way, I had made a search of what was known to me and constructed a pattern on the stimulus that was present (the air conditioner) as if I were actually hearing music from my my radio over the buzz of a refrigerator.

Now let me take the liberty to change pace a little. Within this story several points have been made which will be emphasized more formally and related to reading as thinking. The assertion is that thinking processes (cognition) direct perceptions. For example, a variety of shells on the beach may be seen, but one can be selectively attended to and picked out from a group. A similar phenomenon occurs when learning a new word. Many adults have discovered that once they learn a new word, they find it with surprising frequency the next several days. They appear to hear or read the word repeatedly until it becomes familiar or "old" to them.

Perception is a function of previous experience and is unique to the individual. What is seen or heard is what has become expected to be seen and heard. The cocktail party phenomenon is a good example. Through the buzz of a large gathering, individuals can listen to one conversation and suddenly find themselves aware of someone across the room speaking their name or talking about a movie they have seen or a book they have read. It is as if the individual's thinking processes are monitoring all the stimuli bombarding the ear (or other senses), and when those messages that contain meaning to the individual occur, he becomes consciously aware.

Norman (1969) has stated that Heisenberg said this in another way. Heisenberg suggests that we do not get meaning from the environment, but rather we assign meaning to it. To him, an event has no meaning until the person constructs it. Thus, in the example of the refrigerator and the music, I was accustomed to meaning being impeded in the noises of the environment. When the music was not there but elements similar to music were, I constructed a meaning to conform to my past experiences and expectations. What is being suggested is that an analogy may be drawn between the example of the refrigerator and music and children's language and their thinking or cognitive processes.

Consider another example, one that has been used previously in another context. A second grade teacher was presenting a group of words to her slow group and encouraging children to construct new words by adding different initial consonants. In the jargon, these are called "word families." She presented the familiar *old* and the letter *c* and, after some effort, was able to get the response *cold*. She next presented *f* for *fold* and then *g*. No one volunteered and she said, "I'll give you a hint." She. pointed to her watch, and an eager child responded with *gold*. She then presented the letter *h*. A child who had not responded up to this point said, "I know, I know, *silver*."

This child had been listening, had been paying attention. However, she was unable to respond to what was being required. At the point of the hint, the child misperceived the directions and focused on *gold* and responded with *silver*. The meaning of the instructional situation to that child was in a category of metals, not the functional relationships of the parts of the words.

Often what is remembered is what the individual expects to perceive rather than what is actually perceived. Thinking processes, based on past experiences, guide perceptions. The example given above is similar to one of Goodman's findings. He found that children will change the meaning of a story to actually conform to what they know to be true when the story presents facts that are not accurate. That is, children will remember or alter the facts to conform to their past knowledge rather than to what they actually read.

Bartlett (1958) has stated from his studies of memory that individuals remember things by organizing the items within the framework of their experiences. Thus, memory is also a reconstruction of a particular past experience and is highly idiosyncratic and unique to the individual.

What does all this mean for the education of children who come to classrooms with experiences different from those teachers normally expect? Most teachers are aware that different subgroups speak what has been referred to as nonstandard dialect. So-called black English differs from standard, middle-class English in some unique but consistent and regular patterns. However, when children speak a different form of standard English, the tendency of teachers is to inaccurately perceive the language of the child as inadequate or a sign of low cognitive functioning. There is a possible reason why this is done. As McNeill (1970) points out, most English-speaking children master the phonology and morphology of their language by the age of five or six, a time when most reading instruction begins. Teachers may unwittingly listen for signs of accurate production as an indication of reading readiness. A second reason teachers center on production accuracy may be that young children go through stages of reconstructing and shortening sentences that appear to be similar to the nonstandard form. A three-year-old may say "I go" or "I be gone" as a stage in development; whereas, a black child may say "I done gone" as a normal response in his own language.

In addition, it is known from the work of Slobin (1967), Menyuk (1963), Baratz (1968), and others that the repeated sentence technique is an excellent means of determining the stage of a child's language development. Researchers have found that children will omit portions of a sentence that are beyond their stage of development. This finding is consistent with the point of view stated above that perceptions are constructed on past experiences and knowledge. Omissions are seen as an indication of a lower stage of language development. For example, three-year-olds will eliminate (or omit) the passive, while five-year-olds will not.

In our research over the past five years with rural and inner-city blacks, it has been demonstrated that black inner-city children reconstruct words to conform to their own language when there is an alternate form possible in their nonstandard dialect. If they omit the form, this omission may be conceived to demonstrate delayed development or mental retardation.

An example of one of the sentences may clarify this point. Many black children when asked to repeat the sentence, "I asked him if he did it and he said he didn't do it," repeated it by saying, "I asks him did he did it and he said he didn't did it." These children reconstructed the sentence, with very short delays, to conform to their own language. They repeated the sentence, changing it but maintaining the meaning of what was said.

Five- to six-year-old children from black inner-city schools will reconstruct about 70 percent of the words in sentences they are asked to repeat if there is a different form in their own dialect; rural and city white children will reconstruct a significantly fewer number of words. However, an examination of the number of words omitted (not restructured) from the above-mentioned sentences showed that black inner-city children and white middle-class children omitted about the same number. In contrast, a population of very low-functioning white rural children omitted a significantly greater number of words than either the middle-class or inner-city sample. Thus, it is suggested that black children who reconstruct sentences to conform to their own language are demonstrating an active thinking process. That is, just as children "read" what they know to be true in the same way that adults perceive what they expect to be true (Goodman, 1969), so black children reconstruct what they hear to conform to the consistent elements in their own language.

The capacity humans have to process incoming information is limited and, as was suggested earlier, stimuli are acted upon by thinking processes, and meaning is constructed. The black child who changes the sentence to conform to his language is demonstrating normal cognitive functioning but presenting his product in a dramatically different form. These reconstructions may then be perceived inaccurately by teachers as errors rather than the child's remarkable display of ability to process a different form of language while maintaining meaning. It should be kept in mind that a child's speech is only a sample of his language and thinking. It provides a bit of behavior for the teacher to use in forming an hypothesis about his capabilities. And, it is suggested that the child's reconstructions are examples of an active intelligence for which the teacher may build a strong readiness program. Evidence that the child can reconstruct, rather than omit, would indicate that the child can understand a different form of English. In some cases he may be more able to understand standard English than speakers of standard English are able to understand nonstandard English. Therefore, rather than attempt to change the speech of the child, it may behoove the teacher to master the child's language as well as to provide ample opportunities for him to hear and process standard forms. By so doing, the teacher will provide speakers of nonstandard form with experiences that teach them to recognize the written standard form as well as the oral.

Research has shown that the use of the dictated story technique is excellent for encouraging production as well as determining how extensive a child's language and thinking competencies are. Children who dictate or tell about their art work or home experiences reveal a much more extensive experiential base than most teachers who have worked with poverty youth would suspect initially. Through the use of rhymes, jingles, and songs, the rhythm of middle-class connected discourse can be displayed without devaluing the child's oral production. When a teacher tries to directly change a child's language, he is inadvertently trying to change the child's thinking processes—which is to deny the reality of the child's self-concept and usually causes withdrawal and apathy symptoms which Coleman (1966) and others have demonstrated to be widespread among inner-city youth.

What does all this have to do with reading? Reading is perceived as being essentially a thinking process. As Goodman (1969) states, it is a complex process in which the reader reconstructs a message that is presented in graphic language by a writer. Thus, reading is a reconstruction in which thinking is externally guided by the writer, as Neisser (1967) suggests, as long as the message can be reconstructed (understood) by the reader. The child who reads *gold* as *silver*, the child who reads *boat* as *ship*, or the adult who finds music in the rhythm of an air conditioner is displaying the action of the same basic process—constructing and reconstructing meaning from the stimuli that surrounds him.

References

Baratz, Joan. "Language in the Economically Disadvantaged Child: A Perspective," *American Speech and Hearing Association,* 10 (1968), 143-45 PA, 68, 48, 14508.

Bartlett, F. C. *Thinking.* (New York: Basic Books, 1958.)

Coleman, J. *Equality of Educational Opportunity.* (Washington, D.C.: U.S. Government Printing Office, 1966.)

Gibson, Eleanor. "The Ontogeny of Reading," *American Psychologist,* 26 (1969), 136-43.

Goodman, Kenneth. *A Study of Oral Reading Miscues that Result in Grammatical Re-transformation* (June 1969), USOE, OEG-0-8-070219-2806 (010).

McNeill, D. *The Acquisition of Language.* (New York: Harper and Row, 1970.)

Menyuk, P. "A Preliminary Evaluation of Grammatical Capacity in Children," *Journal of Verbal Learning Behavior,* 2 (1963), 429-99.

Neisser, V. *Cognitive Psychology.* (New York: Appleton-Century-Crofts, 1967.)

Norman, Donald A. *Memory and Attention.* (New York: John Wiley and Sons, 1969.)

Slobin, Dan, Ed. "A Field Manual for Cross-cultural Study of the Acquisition of Communicative Competence." (Second draft, July 1967.)

QUESTIONING LANGUAGE DIFFERENCE INTERFERENCE

JUANITO'S READING PROBLEMS:

Foreign Language Interference and Reading Skill Acquisition

NANCY MODIANO
Catholic University of America

Juanito is a first or second grader. His mother tongue is Spanish, and his ability to understand and speak English is minimal.

There are approximately 5 million non-English speaking school-aged children in the United States, of whom at least 80 percent speak Spanish. The rest speak a great variety of languages, European tongues predominating; relatively small proportions are speakers of Amerind or Eskimo languages or Chinese. (Pena, 1971).

As schools now operate, reading underlies almost all academic activities and, with the exception of a few bilingual programs, this means reading in English. Yet, how can one read in a language he can barely understand, let alone speak?

There are essentially two aspects of what is meant by "able to read." One concentrates on the skills necessary for the translation of the squiggly lines we call writing into meaningful utterances; these are the decoding skills. The other aspect, concerned with recreating the author's intent in the mind of the reader, is reading comprehension. Let us consider each aspect separately.

Foreign language interference in the acquisition of decoding skills

Within the concern for the acquisition of decoding skills there are two major approaches. *The Great Debate* (Chall, 1967) rages between those who favor a "phonics" approach, stressing regularities and rules in sound-symbol correspondencies, and those who favor a more global, "sight-vocabulary" approach, which stresses the visual configuration of words and places a greater reliance upon their meanings. Sometimes only the phonics approach is popularly identified with decoding skills, although advocates of both approaches see theirs as the key to unlocking meaning from writing. The debate rages hot between the two camps; the phonics group seems to have the upper hand just now. Actually both approaches are necessary for the decoding of written symbols, and few instructional programs so stress one as to ignore the other. Without judging the relative merits of either approach, let us look into the effects of foreign language interference on both.

The phonics approach assumes that the child can 1) hear the sounds of the language, 2) recognize each of the letters, and 3) learn to associate each sound with one or a combination of letters.

While most six-year-olds can, with enough time and patient instruction, learn to do each of the above in their mother tongue, they have considerable difficulty in doing any of them in a foreign language. First, all the teacher talk which we call instruction is largely unintelligible in a second language. Meaningful instruction can occur only at a primitive "grunt and point" level, with the child expected to react like a robot or a circus animal responding to the commands of its trainer.

Second, the child is incapable of distinguishing many of the sounds of the foreign language, especially those which do not involve minimal contrasts in his own. Thus, the Spanish speaker has difficulty in distinguishing the vowels in *ship* and *sheep;* the initial consonants appear to be easier for him to hear. The inability of second-language learners to hear many of the sounds of the new language has been recognized by linguists for a long time, but not by most reading teachers. For a particularly good review of recent developments in this field see Ervin-Tripp (1970), Greenberg (1968), and Hall and Robinson (1945). What reading teachers have recognized is something they call "listening ability," which they find relates directly to reading achievement (Cleland and Toussaint, 1963; Plessas, 1963).

Third, the child has difficulty in perceiving written symbols, especially individual letters. As reading is generally taught, the individual letters are presented in relation to words which include their sounds; for the child who cannot hear or understand the words, let alone attach meaning to them, this remains a meaningless, rote procedure. We have long known that an individual perceives and remembers only that which has meaning for him (Bartlett, 1932; Bruner, 1957, 1962; Fantz, 1961; Piaget, 1969; Smith and Dechant, 1961; and Vernon, 1937). Just as the child often has difficulty in distinguishing the words and their sounds, so he often cannot perceive differences in the shapes of the letters themselves. And if he does perceive them, he has difficulty remembering what he has seen (Mewhort, 1967; Mewhort, Merikle, and Bryden, 1969; Reicher, 1969; and Wheeler, 1970).

He encounters great difficulty in learning to read through the phonics approach. It is expected that he be able to hear all of the sounds of the second language as recognized by native speakers of that language, but he can hear only some of those sounds. It is expected that he be able to recognize the symbols with which the language is written, but often he cannot. Nor can he make many of the sound-symbol correspondencies native speakers are expected to learn. Moreover, he can understand only the most primitive of the teacher talk in which instruction is given.

Difficult as it may be for Juanito to learn decoding skills through the phonics approach, it is at least as difficult for him to learn using the sight-vocabulary approach. While there is no expectation that he be able to decipher a word through its individual letters, he is expected to recognize each word through its visual configuration and to attach an appropriate meaning to it (see Ervin, 1961; Loginova, 1962; and Van Krevelen, 1961). Although it has been shown that it is easier for a reader to recognize a word by its global configuration than by an analysis of its letters (Gray, 1956; Makita, 1963), Juanito still will have trouble in recognizing the word when he hears it, it is devoid of meaning, and he often cannot even perceive its shape, let alone attach meaning to it. Moreover, his teacher as with the phonics approach, will be able to communicate with him only at a rudimentary level.

Regardless of the method used to teach decoding skills, Juanito will have great difficulty in learning. In time, with enough urging, he may learn to perceive certain letters and words and, like a robot, to repeat them. More importantly, and independently of the reading lessons, he may begin to learn the new language. It is only when he knows enough of the second language to understand what he is "reading" that he can begin to really decode and to read.

The more he comes into contact with the second language, the more rapidly he is likely to learn it. Thus, those children who are the only non-English speakers in their classes are likely to learn the second language rapidly and are often able to catch up academically with their age-mates within a few years. Children living in heterogeneous neighborhoods where English is an important out-of-school language for them tend to learn it more rapidly than do those who live in ethnically homogeneous neighborhoods. Even the presence of radio and television in the home, when these broadcast only in the national language, is a stimulus for learning. But for those children who live completely isolated from the national language, mastery is a very lengthy process, often taking more than merely the elementary school years.

The longer it takes to learn the second language, the longer it takes to learn to read it. It is a very frustrating experience, one in which the children feel themselves to be stupid, incapable of remembering what on the surface appear to be simple details. Feelings of frustration and worthlessness serve only to further retard the learning of reading. In linguistically isolated communities, the most common response is to drop out of school after only a few years of attendance.

However, when children are taught to decode in their own language, they have less trouble in decoding a second one (Grieve and Taylor, 1952; Modiano, 1968; Orata, 1953). The more the two languages use the same sound-symbol correspondencies, the more this is likely to be true.

Foreign language interference in
reading comprehension

Once Juanito has learned to decode in a foreign language, his troubles are not at an end. He still has to understand what it is he is decoding. For native speakers, two major factors have been found to affect comprehension. Vocabulary accounts for about one-half of the variance; the second factor appears to be some type of verbal intelligence, which some researchers have linked to a knowledge of the structure of the language. There are additional factors, such as attitude, frustration level, and legibility, which also affect comprehension.

If knowledge of vocabulary, the first factor, accounts for about half of reading comprehension, the person who does not know the vocabulary is obviously at a serious disadvantage. This has long been recognized. In 1926 West published a study of Bengali speakers learning academic material in English; he concluded that knowledge of vocabulary was the single most important factor affecting reading comprehension. Since then other studies have further substantiated this point of view (Jan-Tausch, 1962).

The second factor in reading comprehension has been described variously by different researchers. There are those who link it primarily with some aspect of logical reasoning (Anderson, 1949; Davis, 1944, Hunt, 1952, 1957; and Jan-Tausch, 1962). Others have related it more directly to grammatical mastery. As long ago as 1917, Thorndike, in his pioneering study of reading comprehension, stated that reading comprehension is based on word and sentence meaning. Later Langsham (1941) and Hall and Robinson (1945) named the second factor the verbal factor; in further analyses Burt (1949) found that the verbal factor was composed primarily of words in context and words in isolation. Holmes (1954) has gone on to suggest that the second factor is composed of verbal intelligence and the understanding of verbal relationships. More recent empirical studies (Labov, 1970; Levin and Kaplan, 1970; O'Donnell, 1962; Sokhin, 1959; and Weber, 1970) have all shown that the reader depends upon grammatical clues to give meaning to the words and sentences he reads. Obviously, the person reading in a poorly mastered language, ignorant of the subleties and nuances of its structure, is at a serious disadvantage. Stewart (1969) has gone so far as to suggest that it is the imperfect mastery of standard English grammar which lies at the heart of many of the reading problems of speakers of Afro-American English.

Foreign language interference and attitudinal factors

Juanito has great difficulty in learning to read directly in English. Once he learns to decode, he continues to have great problems in understanding what it is he is reading until he learns to understand and speak the second language. He can hardly remain ignorant of how slow his progress is as compared to that of native speakers. In first grade he may have been given a first grade reader; in second and third grades he finds himself receiving lessons from the same book. Moreover, the book is likely to have a big *1* displayed prominently on its front and spine. Juanito knows he is not learning to read as quickly as he "should." He cannot do what his teacher asks of him. He feels frustrated. He is a failure.

That these feelings of frustration and failure directly affect the acquisition of reading skills and comprehension have long been recognized. Some have gone so far as to consider attitudinal factors the single most important element in reading achievement (Gregory, 1965; Groff, 1962; and Sopis, 1965-66). The inherent failure built into learning to read in a foreign language gives rise to negative feelings which serve only to further slow down and complicate the learning process. Moreover, they teach the child that, at best, reading is a disagreeable activity. The influence of the attitudinal factors is seen clearly in the bilingual programs which offer reading instruction first in the mother tongue, so that the frustrations of learning to read in a foreign language are eliminated. The child faces a task no more difficult than that of any other child learning to read in his own language.

The influence of attitudinal factors was illustrated clearly both in the Iloilo project (Orata, 1953) where school-inspired changes occurred much more frequently in the homes of children enrolled in the bilingual classes than in those of children enrolled in the all-English classes; and in Mexico (Modiano, 1968) where school enrollments in general, the enrollment of girls in particular, the reading achievement of the girls, and general levels of adult literacy were all higher in Indian schools offering bilingual education than in those offering instruction only in Spanish.

Summary

How does the use of a foreign language interfere with the acquisition of reading skills? In every way. First of all, the learner can understand only the most rudimentary type of instruction when his teacher speaks in a foreign language. His acquisition of the decoding skills is greatly hampered because he cannot hear many of the sounds and words of the foreign language; he cannot perceive the letters and visual configurations by which the words are represented; and he seldom can link the sounds and the symbols meaningfully. What he learns he learns by rote. The lack of vocabulary and nonmastery of grammatical structures greatly impede his comprehension of what he does read. All of this gives rise to strong feelings of frustration and often of failure, feelings which only serve to further impede the acquisition of reading skills and which tend to alienate the child from school.

References

Anderson, C. C. "A Factorial Analysis of Reading," *British Journal of Educational Psychology*, 19 (1949), 220-21.

Bartlett, F. C. *Remembering*. (Cambridge, Massachusetts: University Press, 1932.)

Bruner, Jerome. "On Perceptual Readiness," *Psychological Review*, 64 (1959), 123-52.

Bruner, Jerome. "Social Psychology and Perception," *The Causes of Behavior*, J. F. Rosenblith and W. Allinsmith, Eds., 363-69. (Boston: Allyn and Bacon, 1962.)

Burt, C. "The Structure of the Mind," *British Journal of Educational Psychology*, 19 (1949), 176-79.

Chall, Jeanne. *Learning to Read: The Great Debate.* (New York: McGraw-Hill, 1967.)

Cleland, Donald L., and Toussaint, Isabella. "The Interrelationship of Reading, Listening, Arithmetic Computation, and Intelligence," *Reading Teacher*, 16 (1963), 252-60.

Davis, Frederick B. "Fundamental Factors of Comprehension in Reading," *Psychometrika*, 9 (1944), 185-97.

Davis, Frederick B. "The Teaching of Comprehension of Reading in the Secondary School," *Education*, 76 (1956), 541-44.

Ervin, Susan M. "Learning and Recall in Bilinguals," *American Journal of Psychology*, 74 (1961), 446-51.

Ervin-Tripp, Susan. "Structure and Process in Language Acquisition," *Report of the 21st Annual Round Table Meeting on Linguistics and Language Studies.* (Washington, D.C.: Georgetown University Press, 1970), 313-44.

Fantz, Robert L. "The Origin of Form Perception," *Scientific American* 204:5 (1961), 66-72, 204.

Gray, William S. *The Teaching of Reading and Writing: An International Survey.* (Paris: UNESCO. Chicago: Scott, Foresman, 1956.)

Greenberg, Joseph H. *Anthropological Linguistics: An Introduction.* (New York: Random House, 1968.)

Gregory, Robin E. "Unsettledness, Maladjustment, and Reading Failure: A Village Study," *British Journal of Educational Psychology*, 35 (1965), 63-68.

Grieve, D. W., and Taylor, A. "Media of Instruction," *Gold Coast Education*, 1 (1952), 36-52.

Groff, Patrick J. "Children's Attitudes Toward Reading and Their Critical Reading Abilities in Four Content-Type Materials," *Journal of Education Research*, 55 (1962), 313-17.

Gudshinsky, Sarah C. *How to Learn an Unwritten Language.* (New York: Holt, Rinehart and Winston, 1967.)

Hall, W. E., and Robinson, F. P. "An Analytic Approach to the Study of Reading Skill," *Journal of Educational Psychology,* 36 (1945), 429-42.

Holmes, Jack A. "Factors Underlying Major Reading Disabilities at the College Level," *Genetic Psychological Monographs,* 49 (1954), 3-95.

Hunt, Lyman C., Jr. "Can We Measure Specific Factors Associated with Reading Comprehension?" *Journal of Education Research,* 51 (1957), 161-72.

Hunt, Lyman C., Jr. "A Further Study of Certain Factors Associated with Reading Comprehension," unpublished doctoral dissertation, Syracuse University, 1952.

Jan-Tausch, James. "Concrete Thinking as a Factor in Reading Comprehension," in J. Allen Figurel (Ed.), *Challenge and Experiment in Reading,* Proceedings of the International Reading Association, 7, 1962. (New York; Scholastic Magazines, 161-64.)

Keane, George R. "The Measurement of Readability," *Encyclopedia of Educational Research* (4th ed.). (New York: Macmillan, 1969.)

Labov, William. "The Reading of the -ed Suffix," *Basic Studies on Reading,* H. Levin and J. P. Williams, Eds., 222-45. (New York: Basic Books, 1970.)

Langram, R. T. "A Factorial Analysis of Reading Ability," *Journal of Experimental Education,* 10 (1941), 57-63.

Levin, Henry, and Kaplan, E. L. "Grammatical Structure and Reading," *Basic Studies on Reading,* H. Levin and J. P. Williams, Eds., 119-33. (New York: Basic Books, 1970.)

Loginova, E. A. "Ovliyanii Interesa Na Zapominanie Novykh Slov Pri Izuchenii Inostrannogo Yazyka (On the Influence of Interest on Remembering New Words During the Study of a Foreign Language)," *Voprosy Psikhologgii,* 1 (1962), 61-64.

Makita, Kiyoshi. "The Rarity of Reading Disability in Japanese Children," *American Journal of Orthopsychiatric,* 38 (1968), 599-614.

Mewhort, D. J. K. "Familiarity of Letter Sequences Response Uncertainty, and the Tachistoscope Recognition Requirement," *Canadian Journal of Psychology,* 21 (1967), 309-21.

Mewhort, D. J. K.; Merikle, P. M.; and Bryden, M. P. "On the Transfer from Iconic to Short-term Memory," *Journal of Experimental Psychology,* 81 (1969), 89-95.

Modiano, Nancy. "Bilingual Education for Children of Linguistic Minorities," *America Indigena,* 28 (1968), 405-14.

O'Donnell, Roy. "Awareness of Grammatical Structure and Reading Comprehension," *High School Journal,* 45 (1962), 184-88.

Orata, Pedro T. "The Iloilo Experiment in Education through the Vernacular," *The Use of Vernacular Languages in Education.* (Paris: UNESCO, 1953), 123-31.

Pena, Albar. Personal Communication (1971).

Piaget, Jean. *The Mechanisms of Perception.* (New York: Basic Books, 1969.)

Plessas, Gus P. "Reading Abilities of High and Low Achievers," *Elementary School Journal,* 63 (1963), 223-26.

Reicher, G. M. "Perceptual Recognition as a Function of Meaningfulness of Stimulus Material," *Journal of Experimental Psychology,* 81 (1969), 275-81.

Smith, Henry E., and Dechant, Emerald V. *Psychology in Teaching Reading.* (Englewood Cliffs, N. J.: Prentice-Hall, 1961.)

Sokhin, F. A. "A Farmirovanii Iazykovykh Obobschschenii v Protsesse Rechevogo Razvitiia (On the Formation of Language Generalization in the Process of Speech Development)," *Voprosy Psikholggii,* 5 (1959), 112-23.

Sopis, Josephine. "The Relationship of Self-Image as Reader to Reading Achievement," *Academic Therapy Quarterly,* 1 (1965-1966), 94-101, 113.

Stewart, William A. "On the Use of Negro Dialect in the Teaching of Reading," *Teaching Black Children to Read,* Joan Baratz and Roger Shuy, Eds., 156-219. (Washington, D.C.: Center for Applied Linguistics, 1969.)

Thorndike, Edward L. "Reading as Reasoning, A Study of Mistakes in Paragraph Reading," *Journal of Educational Psychology*, 8 (1917), 323-32.

Van Krevelen, Alice. "The Relationship Between Recall and Meaningfulness of Motive Related Words," *Journal of Genetic Psychology*, 65 (1961), 229-33.

Vernon, M. D. *Visual Perception*. (Cambridge, Massachusetts; University Press, 1937.)

Weber, Rose-Marie. "First-Graders' Use of Grammatical Context in Reading," *Basic Studies on Reading*, H. Levin and J. P. Williams, Eds., 147-63. (New York: Basic Books, 1970.)

West, Michael. *Bilingualism, with Special Reference to Bengal*. Occasional Reports, 13, Bureau of Education, India. (Calcutta: Government of India Central Publications Branch, 1926.)

Wheeler, D. D. "Processes in Word Recognition," *Cognitive Psychology*, 1 (1970), 59-85.

PROBLEMS IN TEACHING CHILDREN WITH NONSTANDARD DIALECTS

MILDRED R. GLADNEY
Chicago, Illinois, Public Schools

The maturing teacher of today is operating from the position that a number of the problems facing him and the schools stem from his own inadequacies and deficiencies. He sees the criticism directed at him and the schools, both from his colleagues and outsiders, as forceful and positive reasons for taking a critical look at his ideas about children; his ideas about why and how to educate which children; his attitudes about such issues as black/white hostilities, poverty and starving Americans, youth unrest, the Vietnam War; and at his actions, inside and outside of the classroom, which make him relevant to his pupils.

Old and new facts

The maturing teacher asks himself how old are his "facts" about children, how they learn, how they feel about life and their society; about the place of the school in the community, the place of the community in the school; about different ethnic cultures; about what should be taught in school and why. Is he thinking and behaving on the basis of knowledge and principles he learned ten or fifteen years ago? Is there a need for updating his ideas, his behavior?

In this time of great change, old facts, long-held beliefs and opinions, and old ways of doing things must be evaluated and tested against new discoveries both in intellectual fields and from one's own changing experiences.

Classroom teachers, by and large, are not research oriented. They are not prone to use the scientific method to solve problems of the classroom—problems of concept building and skill development, problems of human relations and human rights. Teachers are not trained to deal with new ideas and new theories in intellectual fields; that is, to understand, evaluate, and then, perhaps to change attitudes, to do something differently or to do the same thing with a better understanding of why it is done that way. Not knowing how to deal with new theories and new learnings is one of the deficiencies or inadequacies that the maturing teacher finds in himself.

New and changing ideas also come from the teacher's growing and expanding experiences with his pupils and their community— a rich source for real, pertinent information and insights about the lives, the wants, and the needs of a people who may be strangers to him. Teachers are not trained to be comfortable with differences among people, to accept and utilize these differences that are part of our society. This, too, is a deficiency recognized by the maturing teacher. In order to begin to deal with his teaching/learning problems, the maturing teacher decides he must become a teacher/researcher.

Color/class blindness

A reality of the classroom is that the teacher teaches and interacts with not just a child but also a member of an ethnic group and a social class. The teacher himself is a member of an ethnic group and a social class. If the ethnic and/or class backgrounds of the teacher and the child differ, there is bound to be much that the teacher does not know or understand or accept (consciously or unconsciously) about the child's background, his group and personal lifestyles.

Some teachers may insist that they are color blind and class blind, but the teacher/researcher realizes that it is highly improbable that such blindness exists in the classroom when it does not exist anywhere outside of the classroom in human dealings in this society. He may also question whether such blindness might be, in fact, a cop-out at a time when black people, Indian people, and Mexican-American people are saying, "Recognize us as we are. Deal with us as we are. Put our problems at the top of your priorities for progress toward a better world."

The teacher above all must try to know and understand the various cultural and ethnic groups in this society, particularly if he teaches the children of these various groups. The teacher/researcher must examine his opinions about and feelings toward the black child, the Indian child, the Spanish speaking child. He must seek to find those personal prejudices which interfere with his working and interacting with a child on a basis of respect and affection.

New ideas on language

"How inferior is different?" The speech of many black Americans is seen as being different—both by blacks and others. It has been suggested that this speech is inferior, corrupted; one hears and reads of lazy lips and lazy tongues. Black speech has been viewed as a sign of cognitive deficiency and verbal deprivation. It has been designated as a significant factor in black children's seeming inability to learn to read.

Classroom teachers have failed to teach many black children how to be successful readers. The teacher/researcher begins to examine this problem by asking:

What do I know about language?
What do terms such as *different, inferior, pure, right,* and *wrong* mean in the study of language?
What do I know about this child's language? How does it differ from mine, his classmates?
What does he do with his language; how does he use it? Does it vary from situation to situation?
What do I know about this child's speech and its relation to his potential for reading?
What else do I need to know?

Exploring some of these questions will lead the teacher to the new discussions and discoveries in language, some of which are challenging previously unquestioned principles of learning and behavior. Some that the teacher/researcher will find fruitful indicate that:

1. All human beings learn a language.
2. All language has a system—a set of rules by which the native speaker determines those sentences that are well-formed or "correct" and ill-formed or "noncorrect."
3. The average person is unaware of the linguistic rules of the system from which he speaks. The rules which constitute the person's linguistic system are called his linguistic competency. His linguistic performance or how he behaves linguistically does not always conform to his competency.
4. The child learns his language from those speakers around him; that is, he creates his own linguistic system from the systems of the speakers around him. What he observes is their performance; therefore, he has to continually test data received from them against his own developing set of rules so that his rules can eventually approximate those of the speakers he observes.
5. Dialects of a language are varieties of that language. Most speakers of a language use one or more dialects.
6. A standard dialect is one that has come to be given special prestige for a variety of reasons. It is neither inherently more correct or more adequate than another. Nor is one dialect a corrupt form of another or of the standard language.

Such discussions affirm the native ability and potential of the black child whose dialect is different from the teacher's or the school society's. Because he does speak a dialect of a language, he shows his capabilities to observe language, to process language data, and to create a linguistic system which allows him to communicate with his peers.

Language of black people

What of the child's language background and heritage? Is there a paucity of language within the black community? The teacher/researcher will find the black community is full of

language. It can be observed in the classroom and on the play-
ground. It can be observed in the churches and the meeting
places of the community.

A black child says:

> I have a dream. Dr. Martin Luther King.
> Do you know me? Dr. Martin Luther King.
> I am the President. Dr. Martin Luther King.
> I own this state. Dr. Martin Luther King.
> Meet my brother. Dr. Martin Luther King.

(Scott, 1971)

A black man says:

BLACK OUT

The child psychologist Piaget says that "intelligence is a
particular instance of biological adaptation." *[Origin of Intelligence.]* White people say that intelligence is adapting to their
culture (ask any white person).

I agree with Piaget because I'm a witness to the fact that
Black people adapt to a culture of their own and they also
have the ability to adapt to the harsh white culture.

The beautiful thing about most Blacks is that when they are
forced to adapt to the white culture they can do it without losing
their own culture.

Most Blacks learn how hard life can be at thirteen or three
and they also learn how to maintain their cool. A *cool* is a
facet of the Black culture that tells a Blackman when to get bad
or to lay dead, and all Blackmen try to dig what their *cool* has
to say. (Whites don't have no cool.) A *cool* tells Black people
not to attack whitey without no power because that just ain't
cool. A *cool* tells Black people to enjoy life and watch whitey
kill himself off because he ain't got no kind of cool.

Cool tells the brothers how to rap to the sisters. Cool tells
sisters to dig or to turn back the brothers game. Cool is the
brother's walk, talk, and stalk. Cool is the way he throws them
hands and snows "the man" (the boy). Cool is the way brothers
and sisters jam, causing white folks to pray to their God asking
him to give *them* moves that are poetry in motion.

I have a cool and I dig my cool, but there's one thing about
a cool I don't dig. While Blacks are being cool, whites get credit

for a myriad of things Blacks have done, can do, and will do. Us Black folks don't dig that, but we must dig what our *cool* says for it has kept us alive lots of ways (so we can make "the Black comeback").

Alongside *cool* is *soul,* a term over talked about by whites and having meaning only to Blacks. First I must say whites can be cold, but that's not a *cool* and if you don't have a cool you can't truly understand soul. All you can do is *groove* on its beauty and say what makes those Black folks act soooo coooool.

Soul can't be defined in white terms, but Blacks know how to communicate it amongst themselves. (Like you can't find *"Black Soul"* in Websters.) I can't write/define Soul, so all you non-colored folks will just have to stick to *science* and be *soul/less.*

If you are white and feel *left-out,* don't! Feel *Blacked-out!!!*

(Sanjulu, 1971)

Such emotional and intellectual power has been expressed by black people, orally and in writings, since their beginning days in this country.

The teacher/researcher will have no difficulty finding sources of black language in addition to that provided by his pupils. Black and white publishing companies are printing contemporary and historical writings of black people. Recordings and tapes of black speeches and poetry are available. Educational television and the other networks offer a few black talk shows such as *Black Journal* and *Soul.* Black-oriented radio shows can be heard in a number of communities. The data are here. The teacher/researcher must decide to make use of it.

One of the services linguists can offer teacher/researchers is a description of some of the common features of black dialects. This information adds specifics to the teacher's knowledge of a different dialect. It gives him the opportunity to examine in detail a child's language against a description by experts. From there, he can get some idea of the child's system and developing competence. It should also aid him in choosing more appropriate materials and methods for teaching the child how to read.

Talking, writing, and reading

Having determined some of his gaps of knowledge about the black child and black language, the teacher/researcher poses further questions: If the child performs the complex tasks of learning to talk, does it follow that he can assuredly learn to read? Are there different abilities involved? What are the factors that aided and strengthened his learning to talk that are not working in the reading situation? Can a child refuse to learn to read? When and how does this refusal begin?

Thinking about these questions, the teacher/researcher might decide that the child in school must be allowed and encouraged to use his language freely. He should be helped to expand his language—to add new words, new expressions. His language expressing his ideas and concerns should be listened to, written down, tape recorded, discussed, exhibited, used.

The language of his people should be freely used. Poems on the bulletin board, books and magazines in plentiful number with illustrations that show him and his people, recordings of his people speaking in their dialects—Malcolm X, Martin Luther King, Jr., southern black children, black actors and actresses, people of his community, his school.

Surrounded by language familiar to him—that of his own and that of others—hearing it, seeing it written, feeling free to talk without being criticized for not knowing "how to talk," being encouraged to talk about his ideas, the child can accept as a natural next step the idea of learning to read. Starting with his language in his stories strengthens his belief that he has something worthwhile to say and worthwhile to learn to read. It also convinces him that others have things to say that he will enjoy learning about through reading. The necessary hard work that will come can be accepted because his teacher has respect for his ability to do and will allow him to follow his own timetable.

References and Notes

Sanjulu (Michael C. Randall). "Black Out," unpublished class essay, University of Nebraska at Lincoln, March 1971.

Scott, Dario. Unpublished class poem written at the Elliott School in Lincoln, Nebraska, February 1971.

DIALECT DIFFERENCES IN ORAL READING:

An Analysis of Errors

Rose-Marie Weber
McGill University

This paper is an exercise in the description of oral reading errors. The description has several purposes. First of all, it is intended to show which supposed errors in a given passage have their source in the speech of a group of children who speak Negro nonstandard English (NNE). This calls for the comparison of these children's reading with the performance of a group of speakers of standard English (SE) and requires some reflection on what might constitute an error.

The more general purpose of the description is to demonstrate by way of example the importance of analyzing errors in the context of the sentences in which they occur. As we shall see, the same errors turn up time and again in a given passage as it is read by children from both groups. Even an informal speculative examination of the context of these errors can go a long way toward explaining their recurrence. Furthermore, such analysis may show that some errors are better viewed as positive signs of fluent reading than viewed as unfortunate blunders.

Materials

A 66-word passage was constructed from words frequently found in first grade materials.[1] The passage was presented in the following arrangement, but in primary type:

> I saw the big white dog come.
> He went after my cat. My cat ran away.
> We looked for her on the hill,
> but she was not there.

> The dog ran up to the house.
> Tom let him in.
> "Where is your cat," said Mother.
> "I don't know," I said.
> "She ran away."
> Then something ran down the hill.
> My cat had come back to me!

This selection is not diagnostic in that it was not specifically prepared for demonstrating how speakers of Negro nonstandard English would deal with the points on which their everyday spoken language differs from the written, e.g., -ed past; third person singular -s; plural -s. On the other hand, it is characteristic of early reading material in that most of the verbs are irregular in the past forms (saw, ran), the sentences are short and somewhat disjointed, the characters appear without introduction, and direct quotation comprises a good part of the text.

Procedure and selection of subjects

For this study we sought performances on the passage which included a few errors, but not enough to make it incoherent or to break down the reader's use of contextual cues for proceeding through the passage. We first collected a large number of performances.[2] In each case, the child read the passage at sight in the presence of an adult researcher who provided the correct word if the child paused for about five seconds. Each reading was tape recorded. From this rather large sample, we then selected performances with from 3 to 11 errors. In each dialect group we found 24 children (12 boys and 12 girls) whose errors fell within this range and whose combined total came to 144 (mean 6.0). The data under examination then, are 288 errors made in 48 different oral renditions of the same passage.

One set of 24 performances was drawn from readings by black children from Washington, D.C. On the basis of informal interviews and recordings of the children chatting and reading, it was concluded that these children spoke with features characteristic of Negro nonstandard English. Seventeen of the performances were drawn from readings by 26 children who had been judged competent to read the passage by their teachers; they were in their last month of second grade. In the presence of a black female researcher, they first read a familiar page from their basal text aloud; they then went on to read the above passage. Since 17 children made from 3 to 11 errors (mean 5.9) for a total of 100 errors, they were included in our study. Since the other 9 children made 2 errors or fewer, they were rejected from our study.

Another 7 performances by NNE speakers were drawn from 11 readings by a group of post second graders attending a summer school program. These children were not preselected on grounds of competence, nor did they have the opportunity to practice on familiar materials before reading the passage. A white male researcher tape recorded their performances. Seven of the 11 readings included 3 to 11 errors for a total of 44 (mean 6.3) and so were included in this study. Inspection revealed no differences in error patterns from the first sample by NNE speakers.

The second set of 24 performances on the passage was drawn from readings by white children from suburban and rural classes in the Ithaca, New York, School District during their last month of first grade. Although these children are referred to as speakers of standard English in this study, it must be noted that about a quarter of them regularly used nonstandard features in their speech, e.g., *ain't* and double negatives, but did not share the special features that characterize Negro nonstandard English. White researchers tape recorded 79 performances, which comprised part of a final achievement test. From this group were selected 12 boys and 12 girls who had made 3 to 11 errors and whose grand total matched the 144 made by the black children.

Some remarks on scoring

The basic unit of analysis in this study is the written word (rather than the syllable or letter). The types of errors are the substitution of one word for another, omission of a printed word without pausing, insertion of a word that is not printed in the text, and reversal of the order of words on the page. In this analysis, failures to respond are not counted among the errors.

Dealing with oral reading errors of children who speak a dialect markedly different from the one represented in print calls for some discussion.[3] As a few examples will show, it is not always clear which deviations from a "perfect" oral rendition of a passage should be considered as misreadings, as simple differences in pronunciation, or as translations into the reader's dialect. When a reader says "after" for the written word *away* or "coat" for *cat*, there is no doubt that these responses should be scored as errors. They are clear substitutions of one lexical term for another, resulting in a change of text meaning. On the other hand, when a reader's oral language is ambiguous relative to the language of the text, e.g., he says what sounds like "feels" for *fields* or "dragon" for *dragging*, it may be difficult to decide whether or not these should be scored as errors. Such difficulties arose in the analysis of the black children's responses in this study, e.g., some said "den" for *then* and "look" for *looked*.

But these instances represent differences from the standard of quite distinct proportions. *Then* and *den* are two items in the standard variety whose meaning and grammatical properties would rarely bring them into the same position in a phrase or sentence. Even if pronounced identically, as they might be in NNE, they would not result in an ambiguous sentence. In "Den a big white dog ran up," the item "den" cannot possibly be the noun referring to a lion's retreat. From the point of view of the standard, the pronunciation does not result in a sentence that differs in meaning from "Then a big . . . ," unless it is rejected as complete nonsense. It is reasonable to conclude that saying "den" for *then* does not change the meaning of the sentence.

The case of saying "look" in response to *looked*, however, cannot be similarly dismissed. In standard English, "We look for her on the hill" contrasts with "We looked for her . . .," while in Negro nonstandard English *look* serves to refer to, roughly, both present and past time, covering what requires two forms for other verbs such as *go/went* and *tell/told*. In NNE, the tense marker *-ed* is not required to refer to past time; time otherwise may be signaled by forms such as *last night,* by the strong verbs such as those in the passage (*saw, went, ran*), or it may be inferred from the situation. But in SE, the tense marker *-ed* is obligatory in a context such as in the passage at hand. The response "look" for *looked* changes the meaning of the written word and sentence from the point of view of standard English; from the point of view NNE, it does not.

A couple of other minor problems came up in the passage. First, there is the reading "do not" for *don't.* It does not make for a significant change of meaning. Here the writer has made a stylistic choice; he could have written *do not* if he had cared to. The response may be considered irrelevant to young readers, a failure to recognize the writer's choice, or the reader's rightful choice to set the style in his oral reading. The other problem concerns several instances of /l u k t i d/ for *looked* and of /rænt/ for *ran* in the reading of the black children. In these cases the past is marked twice. Like the pronunciation of "den" for *then,* they are not part of standard English, but they do not change the meaning of the sentence.

Analysis

Two passes through the data are made in this analysis. The first is from the point of view of standard English. In this case, "den" for *then* and /rænt/ for *ran,* are overlooked, but the responses that make for a change of meaning is standard English, such as "look" for *looked,* are considered errors. Then the point of view of speakers of NNE is adopted in order to determine which discrepancies from the standard may not deserve the term error.

The 11 sentences of the passage with the 288 responses analyzed as errors from the point of view of standard English are shown at the end of this chapter. The pooled errors of the speakers of NNE are placed above the text, those of the speakers of SE are placed below. Omissions are indicated by a dash (−); insertions are set between the words of the text; the single reversal is indicated by (~). In the majority of cases, each child made only one error in a given sentence. Adjacent errors made by the same child in a sentence are linked by hyphens. The few nonadjacent errors made by the same child in a single sentence are marked by asterisks. Errors that were immediately corrected by the children themselves are underlined.

Before we go on to the analysis of the errors themselves, it is worth noting several differences between the two groups of children that reflect differences in their grade level rather than in their spoken language. For one thing, the NNE speakers, who were second graders, were prompted by the researchers 15 times when they paused; the SE speakers, who were first graders, were prompted 42 times. Another difference shows up in the overall distribution of errors. The older children's errors tended to cluster on fewer words, while the younger children's were more evenly distributed. A comparison of the 6 most frequently missed words in each group, for instance, shows that they comprise 58 (40 percent) of the older children's total, while those by the younger children comprise 41 (28 percent). Furthermore, the older children made errors on 46 of the words in the passage, while the younger children made errors on 55. We take these differences in distribution to reflect the younger children's greater insecurity about the identity of a word, given its graphic display. Another slight indication of this difference in maturity is the younger children's tendency toward greater variation in response to a given word. To take the clearest example, the list of errors on *went* in Sentence 2 shows that the 5 older children who misread it said "want(s)"; whereas, the younger children gave 5 different stems out of 6 responses. Finally, the older children showed a greater sensitivity to their own performances by correcting 40 percent of their own errors, while the younger ones corrected 22 percent.

The first pass through the data from the point of view of standard English is intended to suggest what features in the text may have led the children to give the particular responses that they did. It is clear from the tables that the errors do not occur evenly across all 66 words in the passage. Since none of the words is infrequent in the language or presents a peculiar spelling-sound correspondence, it is reasonable to search for the source of the errors in the grammar and meaning of the passage.[4] The discussion here is limited to written words that were read incorrectly 8 or more times.

The first section below deals with those words that both groups of children misread in about equal numbers. The other sections deal with those cases in which one group misread at least twice the number of the other. In the listing below, the first numeral indicates the sentence number; the second numeral indicates the order of the word in that sentence.

I. In 7 cases, both groups made a roughly equal number of errors on a given word.

$\frac{1}{2}$ *saw.* The response "was" is expectable here, given the shared letters with *saw*, the high frequency of the word, and the fact that it is a verb that would fit appropriately after the subject *I*. All the other responses are also verbs.

$\frac{1}{3}$ *the.* At the outset of a passage, the indefinite article is ordinarily used to introduce a common noun, so that the 11 responses "a" are predictable. Contrast the other occurrences of *the* in the passage ($\frac{4}{6}$, $\frac{5}{6}$, and $\frac{10}{5}$), which trigger only a total of 2 errors among them.

$\frac{1}{7}$ *come.* Note that all the responses fit appropriately into the preceding context to form a grammatical sentence, although somewhat colloquial to the adult. Compare this instance of *come* with $\frac{11}{4}$.

$\frac{2}{2}$ *went.* All but one of the responses are verbs that appropriately follow the preceding pronoun.

$\frac{5}{5}$ *to.* This omission error suggests that as the children read the sentence, they took the preceding word *up* as a preposition rather than as an adverb. Since two prepositions rarely occur in succession, the readers may not have expected the second and moved ahead to the more likely noun phrase.

$\frac{8}{2}$ *don't*. All the errors are other verbs that appropriately follow *I*, including the stylistic variant *do not*.

$\frac{8}{4}$ *I*. The omission of this pronoun before *said* can be expected because of the frequency of the phrase *said X* after a direct quotation, as in Sentence 7. (Possibly the author avoided *said I* as archaic.) Note that all the omissions are corrected.

II. In 2 cases involving 8 errors or more on a written word, the white children responded incorrectly at least twice as often as the black children.

$\frac{4}{5}$ *on*. Four of the 6 responses are, like the written word, prepositions that relate to place.

$1\frac{1}{4}$ *come*. All but 2 of the 14 errors are *came* in this context after *had;* compare only 4 errors on *come* in Sentence 1.

III. In 4 cases involving 8 or more errors on a written word, the black children responded incorrectly at least twice as often as the white children.

$\frac{4}{1}$ *We*. The response "he" can be defended as more appropriate than the written *We* at this point in the passage. The reference of *we* is not clear, while "he" might refer to either the cat or even the dog.

$\frac{4}{2}$ *looked*. All the responses are "look," that is, identical to the correct response except for the lack of the past marker.

$\frac{7}{1}$ *Where*. All the errors frequently begin sentences; "There" is appropriate to the entire sentence and, in fact, to the passage up to this point.

$\frac{8}{5}$ *said*. As in the case of "look" for *looked*, almost all the responses lack only the indication of tense. Contrast the response "say" here with the one case in the phrase *said Mother* in Sentence 7. Its occurrence with *I* and its position at the end of the sentence may be conditioning factors.

A second pass through the data, but this time from the point of view of Negro nonstandard English, shows that there are a

couple of deviations that were made by a high proportion of the
black children and which can be reasonably traced to their
variety of speech, namely "look" for *looked* (½) and "say" for
said (⅘). Although the past forms of most so-called irregular
verbs like *tell/told* and *read/read* are used in NNE as they would
be in standard English, the past forms of regular verbs that are
spelled with *-ed* such as *looked* are optionally marked for past.
And even though *say/said* falls into the irregular class, *say* turns
out to be used frequently in past time contexts. It can be argued
that from the point of view of the children's norm these responses
do not change the meaning of the sentences. They are not mistakes in reading at all but translations from the text into the
children's spoken variety. Although we see that the response
"look" for *looked* is not limited to the black children, let us sub-
tract the substitutions of "look" for *looked* and "say" for *said* from
the total number of their errors. It is now reduced by 20 (14 percent) and is more in line with our expectations, given the other
signs of maturity that we have noted. These then are the sorts
of "errors" that deflate scores in reading performance unless they
are set aside as having their source in the children's speech.

But if we examine the errors of the standard speakers again,
it seems possible to trace some of their errors to their variety of
speech. Twelve of the responses to *come* in sentence 11 are
"came" in this context after *had*. Perhaps this response reflects
insecurity in the use of the appropriate standard form of *come* as
past participle; perhaps it reflects a more general immaturity in
the use of the past perfect tense of the verb. In other words, this
error may have its source in the difference between the standard
language of adults and the language of 6-year-olds.

A close analysis of errors shows that they may well have their
source in the features that differentiate the spoken language of
the readers from the standard language. Other errors, however,
indicate that the source may be in the difference between what
is written on the page and what practically any speaker of the
language would expect to find there, given his knowledge of the
language. Written language, by its very nature, is different from

spoken language. Written language reduced for pedagogical purposes is especially far from spoken language. By their errors, both groups of children showed how they expected the passage to proceed. They responded with real words—except for one error on $1\frac{1}{5}$. They misread a word in one context but read it correctly in another, showing that they took advantage of the context to shape their responses. And for the most part, their errors conformed to the grammatical and semantic constraints of the preceding structure of the sentence.

		a		
		a		
		a		
	was	a		
	was	a		coming
	was	a		coming
	was -	*a*		came
NNE	say* in	*a*		came*

1. I saw the big white dog come.

SE	was -	a	*dog-with*	came
	was	a	wheat	came
	was	a	winter	came
	see	this	- -	came
	have			

NNE				
		want		
		want		
		want		
	Here	wants		
NNE	I	*wants*	a	coat

2. He went after my cat.

SE				
SE	We	want	for	the cart
	We	wants	for	car
	We - looked -	for*	coat*	
	what	cut		
	had			
	ran			

NNE	
	He
	He
NNE	She

3. My cat ran away.

SE				
SE	The	*cut*	runs	along
	The			after

NNE								
	He							
	He	look						
	He	look						
	He	look						
	He	look						
	He	-look						
	He	-look						
	He	*-look*						
	He	*-look*		him	*come*			
NNE	He*-look		*here*	his	in	a	*hills*	did*

4.   **We looked**   **for her on**   **the hill, but she was**   **not there.**

SE										
SE	But	*He*	look		him	*in*	hut	out	the-wants	now	they
		He	liked		him	in			did*		hear(?)*
		He	looking***		him	along***			saw**		here**
		My			here	up			went		
						an(d?)					
						no					

```
                                        - -
                                        - -
                                        - -
                                        - -
                                        —
                                        - -
                                        —
                                        - -*
                                        —
                                        --   treehouse(?)*
NNE          I        went       —     home
```

5.	The dog ran up to the house.

```
SE   Then   These   big   run   - -   home
                    big   runs  - -
                                —
                                - -
                                —
```

```
                    me
       Tim*         me*
       Tim          me
NNE  And-Tommy  left  her
```

6.	Tom let him in.

```
SE    Tim*    left   Tim* - on
      Tim     light - my   on
      Tim     got
```

```
             There
             There
             There
             There
             There
             There
             There
        Then          his
        Were   are-you          he
NNE     We     are you    kitten say
```

7.	"Where is your cat," said Mother.

```
SE   There        you      kitten
     There*       fo(u)r       she*
                  our
```

```
                                        say
                                        say
                                        say
                                        say
                                        say
                                        say
                                        say
                                        say
                                        say
                              - -       say
                               —
            didn't            - -       say
                               —
            do not            - -       saw
                               —
NNE    - -  thought  care  he  did
        —
```

8. "I don't know," I said.

```
SE         wanted    my    - -
                            —
           do not           - -
                            —
           do not           - -
                            —
           didn't           - -
                            —
           came             - -
                            —
```

```
                Run
                He
NNE    So       He    can    run
```

9.   "She ran away."

```
SE              He
                He
```

```
                Mother
                someone    came
NNE    - -      some       run
        —
```

10.   Then something ran down the hill.

```
SE    The        that        run    to    these
      There      she                up
      They
```

				came		
				came		
				came		
				came		
				came		
			have	*came*		
	But		has	coming		
NNE	I	kitten*	- -	a*		him*

11. My cat had come back to me.

SE	It	*kitten-has-*	came	- back
		he	*came*	black
		and	came	black*
			came	
			came	
			came	
			camc	
			came	
			came	
			came	
			came	
			came	
			some	
			the*	

Notes

1. The passage was prepared by the Project Literacy staff at Cornell University for testing as part of the First Grade Study (Harry Levin and Joanne R. Mitchell, Project Literacy: continuing activities. Final Report, U.S. Office of Education Contract EC-6-10-028, ERIC: ED 040 835).

2. The performances by the white children were recorded by the Project Literacy staff under the direction of Joanne R. Mitchell in 1968. The performances of the black children in Washington were recorded by Carolyn Cunningham under the author's direction as part of research conducted at the Center for Applied Linguistics in 1968, and by Andrew Biemiller, formerly of Cornell University and now of the University of Toronto, who was conducting an informal study at the same time.

3. See William Labov, "Some Sources of Reading Problems for Negro Speakers of Nonstandard English," *Teaching Black Children to Read*, Joan C. Baratz and Roger W. Shuy, Eds., 29-67. (Washington, D.C.: Center for Applied Linguistics, 1969.)

4. On the context of errors see Kenneth S. Goodman, "Analysis of Oral Reading Miscues: Applied Psycholinguistics," *Reading Research Quarterly*, 5 (1969), 9-30; and Rose-Marie Weber, "First Graders' Use of Grammatical Context in Reading," *Basic Studies on Reading*, Harry Levin and Joanna P. Williams, Eds., 147-63. (New York: Basic Books, 1970.)

IS LEARNING TO READ
DIALECT BOUND?

Richard L. Venezky and Robin S. Chapman
Wisconsin Research and Development Center
for Cognitive Learning
Madison, Wisconsin

Among children who are speakers of nonstandard English dialects, there is a disproportionately high percentage of reading failure (Eisenberg, 1966). Although nonstandard speech is regularly tied to lower socioeconomic level and to concomitant deprivations which affect educational achievement, such as nonfamiliarity with the sounds and fixtures of the middle-class world, there remains a nagging possibility that dialect separation by itself is a major cause of reading failure.

The purpose of this paper is to examine the extent to which this hypothesis could be true—that is, the extent to which a child's language patterns per se could affect learning to read. This will be done primarily by examining the skills which the child uses in learning to read, asking in each case whether or not a mismatch between the child's language habits and the language of the reading materials could lead to learning difficulties. From such an analysis we hope to clarify how much of learning to read is potentially dialect bound.

The emphasis in this paper is upon learning to read as a psychological and pedagogical task. Furthermore, it is concerned solely with the teaching of reading to children who speak dialects of English. And finally, it assumes that regardless of how reading is taught to nonstandard speakers, and regardless of whether or not a standard brand of English is also taught, the teacher will always be required to understand the nonstandard speech of her students. By understanding we mean not only comprehension, but also sufficient objective knowledge to discern what is standard and what is nonstandard relative to the particular dialect being spoken. Whatever the implications of this assumption for teacher training, we feel that they apply to all methods and to all teaching—not just reading.

Definition of reading

Reading (for the purposes of this paper) is the translation from writing to a form of language from which the reader already is able to derive meaning. By this definition, reading is restricted to processes involving languages which the reader can communicate with by means other than reading (for all except the deaf and dumb, by speech). In addition, reading depends heavily upon the existing language habits of the reader, perhaps more so for the beginning reader than for the experienced one, but nevertheless, these habits form the base upon which literacy is acquired. For the beginning reader, the form of language mentioned in the definition above is usually overt speech, since this is, for practical reasons, the form of language which is easiest to manipulate in an instructional setting. As basic reading habits are established, the form of language gradually shifts to subvocalized speech, then to a more internal form that we will not attempt to define specifically. The basic assumption here is that many of the same language habits used in listening are available for reading; how they are utilized by the reader depends upon his reading ability and upon the particular reading task. Speed reading and rapid skimming, for example, utilize considerably different language habits than does more deliberate reading.

Besides defining what reading is, it is also necessary as a preliminary to this paper to distinguish between the abilities of the mature reader and the development or acquisition of reading. Reading skills possessed by experienced readers represent goals for the teaching of reading, but they in no way tell us how reading should be taught. That adults may recognize whole words or be able to apply letter-sound relationships on request does not mean that beginning reading must be taught by means of whole words or by means of letter-sound correspondences. How reading should be taught depends upon four factors: 1) the skills which the child brings to the reading task; 2) the learning abilities of the child; 3) the teaching environment, which at a minimum includes teachers, resources, and the society in which the school is placed; and 4) the relationship between writing and speech.

Having established that it is reading acquisition, rather than skilled reading, which we want to consider in relation to nonstandard dialect, we now turn to the question of what skills are required for learning to read in the sense just defined. Three broad areas or prereading skills can be named (Calfee, Chapman, and Venezky, in press): those dealing with visual information, those dealing with auditory information, and those of comprehension. As each skill area is considered, we will ask what implication, if any, the fact of nonstandard dialect might have for skill acquisition—that is, what problems might arise from a mismatch between the child's dialect and the implied dialect of the reading materials.

Visual information skills

Successful letter matching or printed word matching will depend on the child's ability to attend to and remember some dimensions of the visual information at the same time that he ignores other dimensions. Those dimensions which are critical to the decision of *same letter* or *same word* are not identical to those important to decisions about objects; that is, special rules exist for reading which are likely to be acquired only in the context of the reading task. Thus the child must induce or acquire the new rules governing identity of visual form in learning to read; there is no guarantee that previous experience will have provided them.

The dimensions along which letters or words must be the same for a successful match include shape of each letter, orientation of each letter, and ordering of the elements. Color is irrelevant, as is absolute size. The child's attention to shape must later be modified by knowledge of equivalent type fonts and upper or lowercase versions of a letter. In the preschooler's world of objects, in contrast, object matching usually requires that size and shape be identical, and often color, but not that orientation or ordering be equivalent. The end point of visual information processing in the skilled reader is the integration of visual information in larger units, so that word or phrase matching and recognition proceeds quickly and automatically, but skilled processing is dependent on prior mastery of the identity concepts appropriate to word recognition.

The fact that the child speaks a nonstandard dialect is unrelated to this aspect of the reading task. In learning to process print correctly, the only possibility for dialect interference is that which arises indirectly from a failure of the teaching interaction, through the failure to comprehend each other.

Therefore, the visual skills required for reading are not only dialect independent, but they are also culture independent in the negative sense that most children who come to the initial reading task have no prior experience for attending to order and orientation in visual matching, and thus must acquire these skills in learning to read (Davidson, 1934, 1935). That these skills are teachable at the kindergarten level, even to children from the most impoverished areas, indicates also that those children who are taught these skills prior to formal education do not possess an irreversible advantage in visual processing.

Auditory information skills

The second set of skills which are required for learning to read involve such processes as matching sounds in auditory words, attaching sounds to letters and letter sequences, and blending separate sounds and syllables into words. These skills are not generally needed by mature readers who can recognize rapidly whole words and perhaps phrases, but by beginning readers as mechanisms for acquiring rapid word recognition abilities. It is in this learning context that letter-sound correspondences serve their primary function—that of aiding a child both in substantiating the identity of a printed word that he is not sure he has recognized properly by visual cues or by context, and in generating an auditory approximation to a word which is in the child's speaking vocabulary but is unfamiliar. Without the aid of letter-sound generalizations, children would require considerably more adult feedback than they typically do now in learning to read and would become competent readers at a later age. We know from recent studies at the University of Wisconsin that even first grade children who have been taught by methods which de-emphasize letter-sound correspondences generalize by February of the first grade a number of correspondences, including some of the variable ones, and can apply them to generate plausible pronunciations for many one- and two-syllable words which they have never seen before.

To be able to pronounce a word in isolation from its spelling—under the assumption that the desired pronunciation is the one that most closely matches the child's internally generated pronunciation of the same word—the auditory skills mentioned earlier must be acquired: sound matching, letter-sound learning, and blending. Of these, the only one that is susceptible to dialect interference is letter-sound learning, since under rational teaching procedures sound matching and sound blending involve manipulation of sounds and words within the child's oral language abilities. The potential problem in letter-sound learning is the letter-sound correspondences in a reading program, derived for a standard English dialect and expressed on phonemic classes, will map more easily into the phonetics of standard dialects than they will into the phonetics of some nonstandard dialects. But the available data on the phonology of nonstandard dialects indicate that letter-sound correspondences in typical reading programs are no more deviant than for some standard dialects, such as Eastern New England and the Deep South. The reason for this is that most nonstandard phonology differs from standard phonology primarily in differences of phonetic realization of the same spelling, such as mapping the spelling *th* in one dialect into [θ] and into some variant of [t] in another, or in differences of phonotactics, such as leveling final -nd to [n] in one dialect but retaining it as [nd] in another. The first class of differences—those of alternate representations of the same spelling—place the same burden on all speakers, in that a single correspondence is involved. Problems could arise if rhymes which were valid for one dialect but not for another were included in the reading materials, but this problem exists today and can be avoided without too much difficulty, even if it means not using rhymes in the teaching of reading.

The second class of differences—those on the phonotactical level—do not appear to create reading problems. An Eastern New England child, for example, when faced with a spelling like *plarm*, tends to say [pla:m], not [plarm], because in his unconscious phonological habits [plarm] is inappropriate. Therefore, if a child, in both learning and applying letter-sound generalizations, is permitted to map from spelling to his own phonetics, he is at no greater theoretical disadvantage if he speaks a nonstandard dialect than if he speaks some standard ones. And we have no evidence to show that any speaker of English is at a special disadvantage because of the letter-sound correspondences of standard English.

This does not rule out, as mentioned above, pedagogical situations in which the exemplars chosen are not valid for all dialects —such as rhyming or sound matching—but these are not intrinsic to learning to read and can be emended without a basic change in reading materials.

Comprehension skills

The final set of skills we will consider are comprehension skills, by which we mean both the immediate and direct understanding that usually arises in listening to a speaker of one's own dialect and the more reflective understanding arising from integrative, elaborative, or critical thinking triggered by speech or writing. In the absence of evidence to the contrary, we assume that the speaker of a nonstandard dialect is able to understand his fellow dialect speakers as easily as speakers of a standard English dialect understand one another; and, further, equally capable of reflective thinking.

What must be asked, then, is whether existing initial reading materials impose comprehension burdens on nonstandard speakers more so than on standard speakers, and if so, whether this situation can be rectified without resorting to separate materials for each nonstandard dialect. Neither of these questions can be answered definitively, based upon existing data. It is clear that syntactic differences exist between standard and nonstandard dialects, such as in the use of the various forms of the verb *to be*, but the existing data relate almost exclusively to production; there is no corresponding body of data on comprehension, other than that obtained primarily from tasks that are invalid for measuring this variable, such as sentence repetition tasks. Even if we could show a comprehension deficit in nonstandard speakers for certain typical reading materials, we would still have to show both that this deficit interfered with learning to read and that this deficit was greater than that suffered by standard speakers when confronted with the same vapid and emasculated offerings of present-day reading materials. It should be kept in mind that there is a considerable overlap in the experiential background of children everywhere in the world: interactions with parents and peers, receiving gifts, sleeping and eating, observing the weather, and so on. And there is an equally large overlap in the syntax and vocabulary of the various standard and nonstandard dialects of English spoken in the United States. Not all reading passages need concern farm animals, private homes, and a father who returns joyfully from the office at 5:25 every weekday. Whatever may be the reading difficulties caused by present-day readers, there is every reason to assume that within the limited vocabulary range, sentence length, and syntax forms commonly prescribed for initial reading, materials can be developed which are valid for all dialects and cultures within the United States.

Conclusions

From the foregoing analysis we conclude that there is little direct interference of dialect with reading—but an enormous potential for indirect interference. Indirect interference can arise either through the failure of the teacher to recognize what is regular and what is aberrant for a particular dialect and to act accordingly, or through the failure of textbook developers to restrict vocabulary, syntax, and semantics to a common core that is either known already to the majority of the standard and non-standard speakers or can be taught orally within a reasonable time period before reading instruction begins. Given the limitations commonly placed on primary school reading materials, and the small area in which dialects deviate, compared to where they overlap, we cannot find any justification for the enormous expense involved in developing special materials for each group of nonstandard speakers. This money could be more wisely spent in improving teacher training and preschool programs so that by the time nonstandard speakers reach first grade they will not only be better prepared than ever before to learn to read, but they will also enter a learning environment in which the potentially most important variable—the teacher—is capable and willing to teach.

References

Calfee, R. C.; Chapman, R. S.; and Venezky, R. L. "How a Child Needs to Think to Learn to Read," *Cognition in Learning and Memory*, Lee Gregg, Ed. (New York: John Wiley and Sons, in press.)

Davidson, H. P. "A Study of the Confusing Letters *b, d, p, q*," *Journal of Genetic Psychology*, 47 (1935), 458-68.

Davidson, H. P. "A Study of Reversals in Young Children," *Journal of Genetic Psychology*, 45 (1934), 452-64.

Eisenberg, L. "Reading Retardation: I. Psychiatric and Sociologic Aspects," *Pediatrics*, 37 (1966), 352-65.

BLACK ENGLISH PHONOLOGY:
The Question of Reading Interference

Paul Jay Melmed
University of California at Berkeley

Although active and often violent debate has ensued over the nature of the reading problems of black youngsters, one assumption has been advocated by most researchers: there is some degree of interference as a result of previously acquired auditory language. In theory, language is a rule-governed behavior. Thus, when the rules of black English conflict with the rules of standard English, interference occurs. Pioneering work in the discovery of the systematic structure and rule-governed behavior of black English has been done by Baratz and Povich (1967), Bailey (1968), Labov (1968), Henrie (1969), Mitchell-Kernan (1969), Johnson (1969), Baratz and Shuy (1969), and Gumperz (1970).

The assumption held is that the middle-class white child decodes the graphic representation of a familiar language. The disadvantaged black child, however, must first decode the written words and then recode them in his own language before he is able to obtain meaning from the printed page. This added difficulty in learning is called interference.

Although the phoneme patterning of either group of children does not match the graphic presentation in a direct one-to-one correspondence, some contend that the black child has a more complicated task. In the early phases of reading, he must relate his speech to curriculum and instruction which do not consider variations from standard English pronunciation. The black child is baffled by this confusing and arbitrary relationship between unfamiliar sounds and symbols. Furthermore, the teacher who has a vague awareness of linguistic and cultural differences is often led to ambiguities as to whether a particular difficulty is a reading problem, a language problem, or simply a problem of misarticulation.

Two examples which were confusing for the student as well as exasperating for the teacher will illustrate these important points. A second grade pupil asked his experienced reading teacher how to spell [ræt]. "R-A-T," she said. "No, ma'am," he responded, "I don't mean rat mouse, I mean right now." After reading orally a passage about a mother mending a dress, the teacher wanted to contrast the standard English homonyms *sew* and *so*. She asked her class to write *so* in a sentence and then read the sentence aloud. "I don't mean leg," responded one of her pupils. Here the student is reading his own speech from the page, subconsciously making "corrections" where the written word is incorrect in terms of his own language system. In any case, his reading is probably conveying the full intent of the sentence just as well and just as logically as reading it in the teacher's standard English dialect. The problem is one of language phonology and structure and not purely one of decoding symbols. Better techniques and tests for assessment of possible interference in comprehension are sorely needed. It is mandatory also for the teacher to have an adequate knowledge of black English dialect and corresponding standard equivalents.

Until we determine the exact nature of this interference, teachers will continue to misunderstand and thus misinterpret nonstandard pronunciation as reading errors. As a result, reading failure among blacks in our inner-city schools will continue.

Studies of phonological features

Perhaps the most important work in the pronunciation of black English phonology has been begun by Labov, et al. (1968). This study of the sound system of Negro dialect in New York City reveals a battery of homonyms which are nonexistent for standard English speakers, but which may affect the oral and silent reading of black English speakers. Labov cautions that when such homonyms are pronounced, they must not be regarded as reading "mistakes." Rather, these are merely differences in dialect phonology. There are many phonological rules which affect the black child's pronunciation "but not necessarily his understanding of the grammatical signals or his grasp of the underlying lexical forms" (Labov, 1970). Labov classifies the homonyms into five general phonological variables:

Variables	Examples
1. vowel variations	pin-pen
	beer-bear
2. r'lessness	tore-toe
	Paris-pass
3. l'lessness	toll-toe
	tool-two
4. simplification of final consonant clusters	ghost-ghoss
	past-pass
5. weakening of final consonants	road-row
	seat-sea

The findings of studies relevant to the problems of black English phonological interference in reading are far from definitive. Experts in related fields of study are divided on the question of dialect interference in reading; and it is this division that encourages intensive research efforts in this area.

An accurate understanding of the rules of black English is obviously not the entire answer to the problem of teaching reading to inner-city black youngsters. The problems of education in urban schools are too intricately involved with issues of social injustice and cultural differences to yield to a single solution. Nevertheless, an understanding of the relationship of reading to black English phonology is crucial in our attempts to improve reading instruction for inner-city children.

Purpose of the study

An investigation conducted by Melmed (Spring 1970) tested the commonly reported assumption that black English dialect interferes with reading. Subjects for the study were forty-five, lower-socioeconomic third graders in the Emery Unified School District east of San Francisco. Data were collected and analyzed to measure racial group differences on four interrelated variables: auditory discrimination, oral comprehension, black English phonology usage, and silent reading comprehension. The study was limited to the degree to which black English phonology was used. Only those dialect differences from the five types of phonological categories mentioned above were analyzed. More specifically, the following questions were raised and investigated.

1. Do differences exist between racial groups in silent and oral reading comprehension, black English phonology usage, and auditory discrimination ability?

2. Do black subjects have special difficulty in discriminating minimal pairs which may be homonyms in black English but separate words in standard English? Will white subjects and other racial groups have the same difficulty if all items in an auditory discrimination test are black-English-dialect-loaded minimal pairs?

3. Do black children produce these same minimal pairs as homonyms, or do they distinguish them in their speech? Will the white and other groups of children speak each word in these pairs differently from black children?

4. Do significant differences in auditory discrimination and black English dialect usage result in reading interferences? Will black subjects have poorer reading comprehension of the minimal pairs if they do not distinguish these words in their speech?

5. What black English phonological features constitute most of the differences in scores on auditory discrimination, speech production, and reading comprehension tests for all subjects?

6. Do black children actually have a new set of homonyms which interfere with reading? Do certain homonyms reflecting specific sounds cause more difficulty in reading comprehension than do others?

7. Will syntactic clues and contextual clues improve reading comprehension of these black English homonyms?

8. Do black children perform better on oral or silent reading comprehension tests and why?

9. Does the black child's discrimination of standard English forms improve with age? If he is unable to discriminate word pairs in isolation, will his comprehension of spoken standard English be impaired?

10. Do black children read with dialects different from the ones they use in conversational speech?

Test procedures

Each child in grade three was given four tests to determine whether dialect interferes with reading. After careful investigation, selected word pairs reflecting five categories of phonological differences between standard English and black English were chosen. Each child first identified the vocabulary words used for each picture. He then took three individually administered tests and one group test. The first test, Test I, Auditory Discrimination, measured the child's ability to discriminate the differences in minimal pairs, or words which may be homonyms in black English but two separate words in standard English. In this test the child simply pointed to the picture of the word which was prerecorded on audio tape by a young black male.

In Test II, Oral Reading Comprehension, the child read a sentence which contained only one of the words in each pair. He was asked to point to one picture of the pair which contained the concept he had read about. For example, after being shown a picture of *jar* and a picture of *jaw*, the child read a sentence, "Bill broke his jar today." The subject then pointed to one of the picture-pairs. While the child read aloud, each sentence was recorded and later transcribed. This procedure provided the scores for Test III, Black English Phonology Usage.

Test IV, Silent Reading Comprehension, was designed to test the subject's ability to comprehend what he read in short paragraphs. The ratio-cloze technique, in which the child made a choice between two words in the context of what is being read, was used. The same words tested above were tested in Test IV. In addition, two more sets of word pairs were tested in each of the five phonological categories of paragraphs presented. Then the regular classroom teachers administered Test IV in large groups.

Testing for any one class took place at the same time each day. Subjects were assigned randomly to be tested. The two subjects who had been absent from one of the testing sessions were tested with the last classroom during the third day.

All of the testing and recording was done by a seventeen-year-old male high school student and the author. The recorder received all of his formal education in the school district under test and was instructed in oral language and reading for two years by this writer. As a result of his training, he is able to use both formal and informal styles of standard English and black English dialects. At times, this same black male student escorted each child into the test room and conducted the administration of Tests I, II, and III. Thus, a very favorable and low pressure test environment was created. Children were at ease and not threatened by making wrong responses. The young male tester was able to evoke responses from the most reticent children without threatening them or causing the least bit of anxiety. His knowledge of the neighborhood and direct contact with the children gave him an advantage over other adult interviewers. He actually was able to enter into an intimate social relationship with some students. Labov (1969) warns that "the social situation is the most powerful determinant of verbal behavior and that an adult must enter into the right social relation with a child if he wants to find out what a child can do" (p. 64).

It is questionable whether the race, age, and social status of this male tester made a significant difference in the performance of all subjects. Labov (1969, 1970) and Sledd (1969) place a great deal of emphasis on modification of testing techniques to reduce the pressures of culturally determined values and attitudes which interfere with such evaluations. This author's experience in ghetto-area high schools and government programs for high school dropouts leads him to concur with Sledd and Labov. However, this may not be the case with younger elementary school children. For example, when the black male tester was unable to test students in the pilot study, a twenty-seven-year-old white male was used. No noticeable differences in test performance or behavior were discovered by white or black observers. More research is necessary to determine the exact restrictions imposed on students of all ages as they were tested by examiners of different ages, races, and cultural backgrounds.

Overview of data analysis

Observations were simultaneously gathered on four tests for each subject. The results represent four interdependent measures: Test I, Auditory Discrimination; Test II, Oral Reading Comprehension; Test III, Black English Phonology Usage; and Test IV,

TABLE 1. Means and standard deviations of four measured variables on three racial groups

Group	Aud. Discrim.	Oral Reading Comp.	Black English Phonology Usage	Silent Reading Comp.
Observed cell means				
I. Black	27.74	28.39	21.57	71.48
II. White	30.57	28.79	27.14	76.64
III. Others	29.38	28.75	26.89	75.00
Overall means	28.91	28.58	24.24	73.71
Observed cell standard deviations				
I. Black	2.80	1.34	2.71	9.95
II. White	1.70	1.42	2.85	4.40
III. Others	3.20	1.28	2.03	3.38
Overall means	2.80	1.33	3.75	7.58

Silent Reading Comprehension. Thus, because more than one dependent variable was observed, the principal statistical procedure employed was the multivariate analysis of variance for the mean vector of the four tests. In this procedure all four variables were examined simultaneously for possible mean differences across the three racial groups—black, white, and other. When a significant F-score occurred, Scheffé contrasts were used to identify the group whose performance was significantly different.

The mean raw scores and standard deviations for the three groups on each variable are reported in Table 1 and shown in Figure 1. The overall cell mean scores and standard deviations are also reported.

Percent correct

Figure 1. Observed cell-means for all tests.

Variables: 1. Auditory Discrimination
               2. Oral Reading Comprehension
               3. Black English Phonology Usage
               4. Silent Reading Comprehension

Groups: ————— Black
               — —— — White
               . . . . Other

As would be expected, the four variables presented in this study possess many elements in common. Table 2, correlation matrix, illustrates this overlap of information.

These statistics are based on complete data for all subjects. It can be seen that fifty per cent of the computed correlations are significant at the .01 level and one hundred percent are significant at the .05 level. Further observation of Table 2 indicates that auditory discrimination scores correlate higher with dialect phonology than with any other obtained scores. The same is true for both reading tests. Thus, additional support for the validity of the test battery is advanced, for it has been established that these language skills are highly interdependent.

TABLE 2. Matrix of correlation coefficients for four variables on forty-five subjects.

Variable	Aud. Disc.	Oral Read. Comp.	Black English Phon. Usage	Silent Read. Comp.
Aud. Disc.	1.00	.31*	.53**	.37*
Oral Read. Comp.	.31*	1.00	.37*	.39**
Black English Phon. Usage	.53**	.37*	1.00	.42**
Silent Read. Comp.	.37*	.39**	.42**	1.00

*p = .05; **p = .01.

The hypothesis of identical profiles is rejected, and the p value for the overall test battery is less than .0001. The p values for each variable are found in Table 3.

TABLE 3. p values for all four variables

Variable	$p <$	Signif.
1. Auditory Discriminations	.009	(sig.)
2. Oral Reading Comprehension	.64	(n.s.)
3. Black English Phonology Usage	.0001	(sig.)
4. Silent Reading Comprehension	.12	(n.s.)

Reviewing Table 3 with respect to the two reading tests, II and IV, no significant differences were found ($p < .64$; $p < .12$). This clearly suggests that although there are auditory and dialect phonology usage differences within and among the groups of subjects, there are no significant differences in reading comprehension. Reading comprehension does not seem to be impeded

by deviations from standard English phonology. More specifically, although the black subjects demonstrate a greater difference
in auditory discrimination and speech, they show no significant
difference in their ability to comprehend the written word.

Conclusions

From all the information yielded by data on forty-five independent subjects on four variables, the hypothesis of dialect
phonological interference in reading was further analyzed. Discussion of the results is presented below.

1. Concerning racial group differences in the four variables
   under test, significant differences in only two variables
   were found: auditory discrimination ($p < .009$) and black
   English phonology usage ($p < .0001$). There were no significant differences in either oral reading comprehension
   ($p < .64$) or silent reading comprehension ($p < .12$).

2. With respect to the black subjects' ability to auditorily
   discriminate standard English word pairs, analysis revealed that performances by black and white groups were
   significantly different with a set at .01. At the same a level
   there were no significant differences between the blacks
   and others or the whites and others. Clearly, then, with
   dialect-loaded tests, the black group and other group of
   subjects have difficulty discriminating word pairs which
   may be homonyms in black English but separate words in
   standard English.

3. Scheffé contrasts were applied to the question of production of these word pairs in speech. With a again set at
   .01, the black subjects showed significant differences from
   the white and the other subjects. Thus, the black subjects
   do produce these minimal pairs as homonyms, while the
   white and other subjects differentiate the words in their
   speech.

4. Regarding the question of reading interference, then, although the black subjects do significantly differ from the

white and other subjects with respect to auditory discrimination and black English phonology usage, they show no inability to comprehend the written word pairs while reading.

5. Of the five phonological categories tested, there was a general tendency for all subjects to have the greatest difficulty dealing with word pairs composed of differences in *l*'lessness and simplification of final consonant clusters.

6. In reference to specific phonological features which cause the black subjects difficulty in reading comprehension, it was found that these children made as much as 34 percent more errors in words contrasted by vowel variations. There was also difficulty with *l*'lessness and simplification of consonant clusters. Overall, it is concluded that about 16 percent of the word pairs including these three phonological features were actually treated as homonyms by the black subjects.

7. Because syntactic clues and contextual clues were eliminated in sentences containing the word pairs mentioned in 6 above, as much as 70.2 percent more errors were made by the black subjects. It has been shown, then, that such syntactical and contextual clues will greatly improve reading comprehension of standard English word pairs.

8. For the black subjects, there were generally more errors in silent reading than in oral reading. Reasons for this were attributed to language concepts developed, familiar vocabulary, and individualized supportive testing procedures.

9. Regarding the relationship between speaking black English and comprehending standard English, 28.12 percent of the black subjects' speech on these tests was in standard English. Only 12 per cent of these responses corresponded to the subjects' reading comprehension responses, but 21 percent of the errors in speaking standard English forms were on items where the black English form of the word was also mistaken for its standard English homonym. Pro-

nunciation of standard English forms in isolation appears to have little relationship to comprehending identical forms. It would appear that these third graders have had enough exposure to standard English in their everyday activity to aim them in recognition of the printed standard English word. However, black subjects who use black English homonyms in isolation may be confused when they hear these same words in oral production.

10. Finally, in a measure to show whether these black subjects use the same phonological features in oral reading as they do in running speech, it was shown that 28.92 percent of the standard English forms were read in black English and 71 percent were read in standard English. A relatively large amount of speech dialect shift does occur. This flexibility with speech style is probably due to the subject's extended contact with standard English.

Educational implications

There is a wide continuum of dialect variations used by black students, just as there are for whites and other groups of subjects. Thus, the concept of a single black English dialect is not consistent with the data presented above. Furthermore, descriptions of linguistic and dialect feature differences are not sufficient evidence for suggesting that these differences interfere with reading and learning standard English material.

In general, the subjects in this study comprehend standard English in written form quite well. They also spoke standard English over 70 percent of the time. Thus, on the basis of these findings, a case for teaching standard English to black English speakers before teaching reading is not justified. In addition, a case cannot be made for translating standard English texts into black English phonology for beginning readers. Rather, it seems that standard English texts can adequately be used to teach black English speakers to read.

On the basis of the analysis of the test data, it has been established that several sets of homonyms existed for the black subjects which were separate words for the other subjects. Reading specialists and classroom teachers must understand, however, that the child's ability to identify the presence or absence of a phonetic distinction is more important than his ability to articulate phonemes in a manner different from standard English. For example, teachers must determine whether the child can contrast the words *past* and *pass* rather than listen for the child to weaken the final consonant cluster -*st*.

Using the categories mentioned in this study, it would be helpful to focus on word pairs which are not distinguished by black-English speakers. Accentuating phonological differences whenever they occur should be avoided. However, if attention to dialect differences seems desirable for a particular group of students, the most common differences between standard English and black English should be systematically studied and contrasted.

Time would be better spent, however, on concept and vocabulary development. Learning to read and reading for meaning should be the primary goals of elementary curriculum programs. Changing speech dialect to standard English pronunciations is a project which should be separated from these goals.

The data clearly show that these homonyms unique to black English (e.g., *toll-toe, road-row*) cause reading comprehension interference only when there is a lack of syntactical or content clues in the sentence. Thus, once a list of word pairs which cannot be auditorily discriminated by the black child has been established, it is imperative for sentences to include enough contextual clues to facilitate the comprehension of these words. Sentences which are ambiguous, in which either word in a homonym pair may occupy the same syntactic slot, should be avoided. To illustrate this point, consider the following example:

1. His (pass-past) made him famous.
2. His perfect (pass-past) to the man in the end zone made his famous.

Sentence 2 would reduce confusion and reading interference because contextual clues in addition to a phonetic contrast are provided. These additional clues should also be present when listening to and comprehending oral forms are desired. In other words, avoid using black English homonyms in isolation, because black English phonology appears to cause interference only where comprehension requires the recognition of phonological clues alone.

Reading and language instruction is more than teaching children a standard language style or moving the students from texts written in their own vernacular to standard English texts. It is more than avoiding the use of certain categories of black English phonological and syntactical features in isolation. Teachers themselves must be schooled in linguistic as well as social and ethnographic characteristics of speech behavior. After diagnosing their own speech behavior, teachers will become more cognizant of their attitudes toward deviant speech. This is necessary because teachers who genuinely do not understand the speech of black pupils may appear to be hostile to dialect differences. Some students interpret an honest, noncondescending question such as "What did you just say?" as a hostile challenge. Because the child is accustomed to having black and white adults respond disapprovingly to his talking, he views the teacher's questions as a reprimand. Or the student may simply feel that the teacher doesn't listen closely because he isn't really concerned. In any event, the understanding of black English features, the appreciation of black culture and language tradition, and an awareness of the intricate interaction between the speaker and the speech situation must all enter into decisions made while black children learn to read.

These important foundations of the black child's speech must also be considered while testing for speech and reading competencies. It is essential to set up and maintain an appropriate social relationship with the child before and during test administration. This may be facilitated by using testers who are intimately familiar with the background, culture, and environment of the subjects under test. Several students who attend local high schools may be trained to administer reading and language arts tests. Their seemingly natural expertise in relating to and communicating with younger students in the community may make noticeable differences in test performance.

References

Aarons, A. C.; Gordon, Barbara; and Stewart, W. A., Eds. "Linguistic Cultural Differences and American Education," *Florida FL Reporter,* 7 (1969), 9-12.

Bailey, B. L. "Some Aspects of the Impact of Linguistics on Language Teaching in Disadvantaged Communities," *Elementary English,* 45 (1968), 570-626.

Baratz, Joan C. "Teaching Reading in an Urban Negro School System," *Teaching Black Children to Read,* Joan Baratz and Roger Shuy, Eds., 92-116. (Washington, D.C.: Center for Applied Linguistics, 1969.)

Baratz, Joan C., and Povich, E. *Grammatical Constructions in the Language of the Negro Preschool Child.* ASHA paper, 1967.

Bereiter, C., and Engelmann, S. *Teaching Disadvantaged Children in the Preschool.* (Englewood Cliffs, N.J.: Prentice-Hall, 1966.)

Goodman, K. S. "The Language the Children Bring to School: How to Build on It," *Grade Teacher,* 86 (1969), 135-39.

Gumperz, J. J. *Verbal Strategies in Multilingual Communication.* Working Paper No. 36, Language-Behavior Laboratory, University of California, Berkeley, June 1970.

Henrie, S. N. *A Study of Verb Phrases Used by Five Year Old Nonstandard Negro English Speaking Children.* (Unpublished doctoral dissertation, University of California, Berkeley, 1969.)

Hess, R. D., and Shipman, Virginia. "Early Blocks to Children's Learning," *Children,* 12 (1965), 189-94.

Jensen, A. R. "How Much Can We Boost IQ and Scholastic Achievement?" *Harvard Educational Review,* 39 (1969), 1-123.

Johnson, K. "Pedagogical Problems of Using Second Language Techniques for Teaching Standard English to Speakers of Nonstandard Dialect," *Florida FL Reporter,* 7 (1969), 78-154.

Labov, W. "Language Characteristics—Blacks," *Reading for the Disadvantaged: Problems of Linguistically Different Learners,* T. D. Horn, Ed., 139-57. (New York: Harcourt, Brace and World, 1970.)

Labov, W. "Some Sources of Reading Problems for Negro Speakers of Non-standard English," *New Directions in Elementary English*, A. Frazier, Ed., 140-67. (Champaign, Illinois: National Council of Teachers of English, 1967.) Also in J. Baratz and R. Shuy, Eds. *Teaching Black Children to Read.* (Washington, D.C.: Center for Applied Linguistics, 1969.)

Labov, W. "The Logic of Non-standard English," *Florida FL Reporter*, 7 (1969), 60-169.

Labov, W., et al. *A Study of the Non-standard English of Negro and Puerto Rican Speakers in New York City.* Final Report, U.S. Office of Education Cooperative Research Project No. 3288, Vols., I and II. Washington, D.C.: Center for Applied Linguistics, 1969.)

McDavid, R. "Dialectology and the Teaching of Reading," *Teaching Black Children to Read*, Joan Baratz and Roger Shuy, Eds., 1-13. (Washington, D.C.: Center for Applied Linguistics, 1969.)

Mitchell-Kernan, C. *Language Behavior in a Black Urban Community.* (Unpublished doctoral dissertation, University of California, Berkeley, 1969.) Also Working Paper No. 23, Language-Behavior Research Laboratory, University of California, Berkeley, 1969.

Ruddell, R. B. *The Effect of Four Programs of Reading Instruction with Varying Emphasis on the Regularity of Grapheme-Phoneme Correspondences and the Relation of Language Structure to Meaning on Achievement in First Grade Reading.* U.S. Department of Health, Education and Welfare, Office of Education, Cooperative Research Project No. 2699, 1965.

Sledd, J. "Bi-dialectalism: The Linguistics of White Supremacy," *English Journal*, 58 (1969), 176-84.

Stewart, W. "Observations on the Problems of Defining Negro Dialects," paper read at National Council of Teachers of English meeting, Washington, D.C., 1966.

Wolfram, W., and Fasold, R. "Toward Reading Materials for Speakers of Black English," *Teaching Black Children to Read*, Joan Baratz and Roger Shuy, Eds., 138-55. (Washington, D.C.: Center for Applied Linguistics, 1969.)

READING, LANGUAGE, AND NONSTANDARD DIALECTS:

A Research Report

RICHARD RYSTROM
University of Georgia

Before describing and commenting upon my work in the areas of reading, language, and nonstandard dialects during the past several years, it is appropriate to point out that a researcher does not prove hypotheses; by carefully choosing and following a research design, and by using appropriate statistical methods, he hopes to control variables in such a way that those he wants to examine will cause particular changes in behavior at the end of the experiment. Since he can never be absolutely certain he has controlled all of these factors, his conclusions must be considered as new, improved, more sophisticated hypotheses. The research conclusions presented below should be regarded as educated guesses rather than facts.

First, the speech habits of most blacks are demonstrably different from the speech habits of most whites. However, a speaker's dialect is not a completely reliable predictor of his race; also, members of any race speak different dialects. Despite these idiosyncratic, social, regional, and cultural dialect differences, there are dialectal features which can normally be used to discriminate between black and white speakers. The Rystrom Dialect Test (1969) was written in order to eliminate the biases of the response evaluator in measuring these dialect differences. From a list of several hundred sentence pairs, twenty-four pairs— exactly alike except for a particular dialect feature in a particular environment—were selected because they most effectively discriminated black speech from white speech. A typical sentence pair was: The sky clouded over; The sky's clouded over. In most cases each sentence with the extra feature was selected and recorded on a master tape, followed by a blank space in which the child was to repeat the sentence he heard. His responses were taped on a second recorder, which did not record the stimulus sentences. The evaluator was given a page with the twenty-four sentence pairs and the recording with only the response sentences; she was instructed to mark the sentence from each pair she heard. Since she did not know which sentence from each pair the child had heard, she was not biased by the stimulus sentences on the master tape. This test indicated significant differences between black and white speech habits. Although the test was constructed in order to produce a greater number of correct responses by white subjects, a similar test could be constructed which would favor the responses of black children. The implication is clear: the test indicates differences in dialect, but it does not demonstrate that black speech is inferior or that black children speak a nonstandard dialect, unless *nonstandard* simply means *different*.

Another study (Rystrom, *in progress*) provides additional evidence of differences between black and white speech. Seventy-two sentences were constructed in such a way that a particular response is dependent upon a child's ability to understand the meaning of a single structure word as it affects the meaning of the sentence in which it occurs. For example: "You cannot sit down *until* you walk around the chair. Sit down." The vocabulary and syntax were made as simple and straightforward as possible in order to be certain the child's response would depend upon his understanding of the word being tested: *until* in this case. While it is too early to derive "new, improved, more sophisticated hypotheses," the most significant difference noted so far is between the performance of black and white children. Black children may learn these sentence structures later, or they may employ different syntactic units to signify the same deep structures. There were no differences between male and female subjects nor between preschoolers and first graders (the age difference between these two groups was approximately one and one-half years).

Additional research projects, using the Dialect Test (Rystrom, 1969) as one of the criterion measures, suggest a second conclusion: black children do not experience difficulty in learning to read because of the dialect they speak. After eight weeks of training, the California children (Rystrom, 1968) in the experimental and control groups evidenced no differences in their ability to use selected features of white speech. Nor were there significant intergroup differences in their ability to read sight words or sight words with controlled phoneme-grapheme correspondences. This study was later replicated in Georgia (Rystrom, 1970) with a larger sample and several other alterations in research design: the dialect training time was increased to half a year; the training was conducted by both black and white speakers, who were also the regular classroom teachers; and the dialect materials were revised. While significant differences were noted in this research, they indicated that dialect training interferes in the reading acquisition process. The children who were given dialect training had significantly lower scores on the word reading test than the children who received no dialect training. After dialect training, children could apparently hear a phoneme they would not normally produce and had to learn to associate it with a grapheme they had learned to ignore. The other significant differences between groups can be attributed to an uncommonly energetic and inventive teacher.

These studies indirectly support the hypothesis that reading is a decoding-recoding-encoding process. Using both his knowledge of sentence structure and linguistic probability, a child can often "read" the next word in a sentence by guessing. When he has begun to associate phonemes with graphemes, when he can respond to the orthographic pattern of the word in addition to its syntactic/semantic content, he can mentally sound out the word. Since the orthographic features of a word only approximate the corresponding phonemes in his dialect for that word, he must recode, or translate the word into his dialect. That is, he might have to change printed *a-s-k* into phonemic /aeks/, the correct pronunciation in his dialect for this item. Finally, he is ready to read this vocabulary item aloud. He can change print into the particular idiosyncratic, social, regional, cultural dialect he knows.

The research described in this paper indicates that the language behavior of blacks is significantly different from the language behavior of whites, but it does not indicate that the black dialect is a less efficient vehicle for learning to read; further, none of the data suggest that speaking a black dialect results in cognitive deficiency. Other researchers have, however, collected abundant evidence to suggest that the reading performance of black students is often below the level of white students. In order to examine possible causes of this reading performance difference as part of a larger experiment (Rystrom and Cowart, in press) a black teacher and a white teacher were asked to give a simple sight word test to randomly selected groups of black and white second graders. The black teacher tested both black and white children, and the white teacher also tested black and white children. When the test performance of these four groups was analyzed, the only significant difference was the performance of the black subjects evaluated by the white teacher. The white teacher appears to have discriminated against the responses of black children because she was not familiar with the range or extent of dialect variation that is acceptable in black speech. The third conclusion: many of the differences in reading behavior noted between blacks and whites may exist only in the perceptions of white teachers who evaluate responses in the black dialect; white teachers who have black students should learn how to understand and evaluate the speech of black children.

Another study suggests that remedial readers in primary grades can be taught to read if specific objectives are carefully defined and taught. In this experiment (Rystrom, in press), a group of black second graders with the lowest achievement test scores and lowest teacher evaluations was given instruction during the school year in multiple-form letter discrimination tasks and in decoding words with regular phoneme-grapheme correspondences. By the end of the year, the experimental group could do significantly better at naming letters than an average-ability-and-performance-level control group; the experimental group also achieved higher word reading scores than the control group, although these scores were not statistically significant.

The results of my research examining interactions between reading and the black dialect can be summarized by the following conclusions: 1) there are measurable differences between black speech and white speech; 2) however, many of the apparent differences between these dialects are misperceptions by white teachers who are not sufficiently familiar with the black dialect to either understand or evaluate responses in black speech; 3) speaking a black dialect does not cause reading failure; 4) black remedial students can be taught to read. If we can eliminate our own linguistic biases, we may find that many of the problems in teaching black children to read will disappear.

References

Rystrom, Richard. *Analysis of Black Syntax.* (In progress.)

Rystrom, Richard. "Dialect Training and Reading: A Further Look," *Reading Research Quarterly,* 5 (1970), 581-99.

Rystrom, Richard. *The Effects of Standard Dialect Training on Negro First-Graders Being Taught to Read.* U.S. Office of Education Final Report of Project 8-I-053, 1968.

Rystrom, Richard. *Teaching Remedial Reading to Black Children: Some Results.* (In press.)

Rystrom, Richard. "Testing Negro Standard English Dialect Differences," *Reading Research Quarterly,* 4 (1969), 500-11.

Rystrom, Richard, and Cowart, Harry. *Black Reading "Errors" or White Teacher Biases?* (In press.)

DIALECT AND THE
READING PROCESS

CAROLYN BURKE
Indiana University

As children, one of our first linguistic lessons involved selectivity. We learned to separate language from noise, to focus on stressed items, to limit our own sound output to the variety of sounds which we heard around us, to focus on the linguistic features and not upon the minor variations caused by different speakers.

This same lesson of selectivity is carried over into social awareness when we recognize our group's chosen way of saying things as opposed to others' ways. Much of our life is, in fact, based upon determinations to selectively classify information. We learn this lesson so well that we sometimes find it hard to perceive alternate acceptable arrangements.

Our initial reactions to and concerns about the effects of various oral dialects on the process of learning to read would seem to stem more from our own predispositions toward a particular language organization than from any linguistic restraints. Many of the difficulties which children face in learning to read are not related to limitations which their dialect creates, but which their reading program imposes.

Nor is it enough to note the differences which can be tallied between a child's spoken dialect and the book's dialect and equate that difference as the actual distance which the child must travel in handling the text. The linguistic circumstance which mitigates this distance is the fact that reading is a receptive language process which makes use of a well-developed system of redundant cueing.

Over the past several years the staff of Reading Miscue Research Center at Wayne State University has tape recorded and analysed the oral reading of some 300 children of varying reading achievement in and around the city of Detroit. Most of these children have been speakers of a dialect other than the one which the school imposes. It is from their reading experiences that examples are drawn.

These reading experiences reflect the effects of dialect upon the reading process when that process is meaning-centered and uninterrupted. The reader has fully available to him the total context of the material and the redundant linguistic cues to both syntax and semantics. At the same time he is left entirely to his own linguistic resources, receiving neither prompting nor instruction from the researcher.

Phonemic involvement

Phonemic level variations compose by far the greatest percentage of dialect related miscues in oral reading. They are the most immediately perceived, the most strident to selectively trained ears. They have received the focus of recent efforts at improving the teaching of reading, a fact to which the long list of phonically oriented "linguistic" readers can attest.

Samples of phonemic level variations are easy to come by:

/cɔ̌w/   call
/dɑ/   the
/skʊ/   school
/wif/   with
/brəfis/   breakfast
/ɑh/   I
/fɑwt/   fault
/laybɑriy/   library
/æks/   ask

What is not so clear is the role that these variations play in the reading process.

Phonemic level variations are not limited to any small, easily identifiable segments of the population. Within the Detroit area such usages as:

Harry will /git/ the ball.

I took a quick step backwards.

He went /əcrast/ the street.

cut across social class and dialect lines. And no one ever raises the question of whether these variations hamper the reader.

Every day in schools across the country teachers dictate spelling words. The teacher says /Tyʊwzdey/; the student writes *T-u-e-s-d-a-y* and calls it /Tʊzdey/. The teacher says /hæv/; the student writes *h-a-v-e* and calls it /hiv/.

Every day speakers of a standard dialect read sentences like the following two:

Tom /æn/ Betty were both from New York.

Bread /ən/ butter was all he had to eat.

They never question the fact that their pronunciation for the conjunction was different in each case and that neither represented the /ænd/ produced when list stress is used. Nor do they question the fact that this item will retain a standard spelling regardless of the various morpho-phonemic representations it might have.

In many of these cases the participants are unaware of or unconcerned over the slight phonemic differences involved. Their lack of concern does not stem from the fact that these differences are any less linguistically distinct than /pin/ or /pen/ for *p-e-n* or /wiθ/ or /wif/ for *w-i-t-h* but because they are not used as social markers. The issue seems to be not whether there are phonemic differences but whether or not those differences cut across socially established dialect boundaries.

Reading, as a process, is usually silent. The phonemic system of the author is irrelevant. Whatever phonemic-level word attack occurs is based upon the reader's system. This is well illustrated by considering poetry—one of the few written forms which is meant to be read aloud. Poetry frequently alters the usual focus and places the reader under the restraint of using the author's phonemic system. The reader can find himself called upon to rhyme *windowpane* with *again* or *been* with *seen,* when for him the natural pattern would be to rhyme *been* with *again.*

In some reading programs the phonemic system of the author is tightly controlled, and the children's attack upon unknown items is strenuously limited to use of that specified form. *He went to the store* /fər/ *a pound of butter* is rejected, not because it fails to make semantic or syntactic sense but because it does not make use of the instructional system being imposed.

The child who successfully applies the system to unknown items can produce /tɛn/ for the item *t-e-n* and not necessarily arrive at the idea that this is identical to his morpheme /tin/ (meaning a number which is one greater than nine). If the teacher concentrates her efforts on the sound patterns involved and not upon the message, she can be blissfully unaware that the item has no semantic content for the reader.

To fully appreciate the situation in which we have placed these children, just imagine extending the phonemic restrictions of some poetry forms to all oral reading and all sound-related word attack. The acceptable phonemic pattern for any piece of material will be based upon the author's dialect. So, if Shaw is the author we must read *It* /æz/ /biyn/ *in the* /la bór ə tor iy/. If Joyce Carol Oates is the author, we read It /hæz/ /ben/ in the /læb rə tor iy/.

No phonemic-level dialect substitution causes either a semantic or syntactic change in the material being read. The reader demonstrates this fact by supplying, in one-to-one correspondence, his oral alternate for the item. In a silent reading situation no text alteration can be said to have occurred.

Reading as a psycholinguistic process involves both anticipating text and confirming one's guesses. In evaluating the effect of individual dialect variations, we must apply the same two criteria which the reader himself uses:

> Is the structure syntactically and/or semantically acceptable?
>
> Is the structure syntactically and/or semantically changed?

In initial reading programs we have tended to center our attention upon that feature of dialect which is the most noisy and yet the least disruptive of the reading process—phonemic variation.

Lexical involvement

Lexical dialect items for speech are numerous:

> greens/salad
> faucet/spigot
> bag/sack
> skillet/frying pan
> pop/soda
> family/kin

They are reliable indicators of such things as the geographic and/or social placement of the speaker. As such, they appear, of linguistic necessity, in his writing. The reader's response to such lexical variations is to substitute his own preferred dialect synonym.

bucket

He filled the pail with water.

they

It was their house.

them

It's growing in the woods across the bay

gym shoes

He put on his sneakers.

further

A little farther, and I saw a button.

gal

Well, Peggy old girl.

out loud

I went on reading the words aloud.

A number of children in our research project read a short story by the English author, Roald Dahl, in which word-level dialect preference became very obvious.

> Both *lamps* and *moment* appeared multiple times in the text.

> I switched off the headlamps of the car.
> The beam of a headlamp shone through the window.
> Wait a moment, Timber.
> Harry paused and was silent for a few moments.

Almost without exception, and regardless of varying dialects, these young Americans substituted *lights* for *lamps* and *minute* for *moment*.

As was the case with phonemic level dialect variations, such substitutions do not cause any semantic or syntactic changes in the text. They simply result from the natural reading process of text anticipation.

In those cases where the reader either has no avavilable synonym or fails to make use of one, for an item not within his dialect he usually reverts to phonemic or graphic attack. In such cases *a typical baby* can be read a *type+ical baby*, the *Civil War* can be read the *Silver War*. As numbers of our readers have substantiated, even these production difficulties cannot be taken as absolute evidence of comprehension loss. *Plain old average* and *everyday* are just two of the definitions given by children who produced *type+ical*.

Structural involvement

Examination of structural-level miscues produces such immediate examples as:

> Then the man lift(ed) his gun to his shoulder.

> "I haven't been bit(ten)," he whispered.

> This (is) all I(ve) got for you tonight.

> Just about everybody like(s)candy.

        gots
        I have a car.

        Then he noticed that this one(s) leg was broken.

The variations are limited and highly predictable manipulations of the inflectional and marker systems of English. And again when we apply our test, there has been no change of meaning. There has been only a simple alteration of the surface-level grammatical structures.

Some of the structural-level dialect miscues of these readers are hybrids, devised out of the interuse of several language patterns. They reflect not confusion over the existence of these organizations but confusion concerning only the limits of their application.

Again, many of these derived forms center around use of inflectional systems.

        deers
      All deer look alike.

        sheeps
      The sheep were in the bedding ground.

                       sung
      He was no longer shy as he sang his song.

        helped+ed
      She helped him find his package.

        throwed
      He threw the ball to first base.

In some cases the reader finds himself dealing with a structure which does not exist within his dialect and is forced to select from appropriate available structures. "He hung up the two telephones into which he'd been talking," a structure which involves past completed action was rendered by one reader as "He hung up the two telephones into which he be talking," which makes the telephone talking an habitual action.

Not all aspects of a child's oral dialect are reflected in his reading. Sentence samples from the conversation of these same children reflect much more distinct dialect variation than is indicated during their reading.

> His class *they* was having an outside project.
>
> To settle the baby down *for stop crying* he just read some S's or some words that start with S *out the dictionary* and the baby went to sleep.
>
> The baby *he* said some new word (plural).
>
> He sang a song *and see would* the deer come to him.
>
> Mr. Bradley had him *to come* down there.
>
> Billy want (past tense) to save *he* deer.
>
> *Their* winter house was a cabin and *they* summer house was a tent.

Not only is increased variation indicated in these samples, but so is apparent dialect inconsistency. All plural or past tense endings are not left off, reflective pronouns do not regularly follow nouns. Within the same sentence a speaker has produced *their winter house* and *they summer house*.

This language flexibility is really the mark of the urban dweller. The dialect research which Roger Shuy and his colleagues conducted in the Detroit area indicated that dialect variables could not be treated as absolutes but only by the frequency of their occurrence in the language of specified groups. All of the dialect variables measured crossed social class, race, and educational boundaries. It is not surprising, then, that this language flexibility is brought to the reading process.

The dialect examples coming from our reading research are familiar to the point of boredom, limited in kind, and cause little or no semantic or syntactic text alteration. That is, they have little linguistic effect upon the reading process. The truly disruptive breakdowns in process come when any reader encounters totally unfamiliar structures.

In a social studies exercise, a third grade boy was asked to complete the sentence "The pony express was discontinued because of (blank)." He produced ". . . *because of the continent.*"

Asked to substantiate his response he referred to two text sentences;

> Then telegraphic lines were stretched across
> the continent. The pony express was discontinued.

How do you explain the fact that he was able to find the necessary text and yet was unable to produce the correct answer? Is he lazy? or careless?

There is at least one available linguistic explanation. The reader was unfamiliar with the syntactic relationship involved and mistook it for another.

If the text sentences had read "John threw the ball. The window was broken," the answer to the question "What broke the window?" would have been the direct object from the first sentence, "the ball."

This reader will be unable to attach semantic sense to these structures until he is able to handle the syntactic relationships involved. He must add this structural pattern to those which he already controls.

Dialects involve reasonably predictable differences between the language systems of people. In this very real linguistic sense, dialect variations face every reader. None of us needs to abandon our dialect in order to become a reader. As receivers of language we all learn to recognize alternate forms even though we might never make use of them in language production. The key is not language change but language growth and flexibility. Perhaps the most impressive aspect of dialect involvement in oral reading is its paucity at the morphemic and structural levels.

References

Burke, C. L., and Goodman, Y. "Do They Read What They Speak?" *Grade Teacher*, 86 (1969), 144, 146-48, 150.

Burke, C. L., and Goodman, K. S. *Study of Children's Behavior While Reading Orally*. Final report, March 1968, Project No. S425, Contract No. oe-6-10-136, United States Department of Health Education, and Welfare, Office of Education.

Burke, C. L., and Goodman, K. S. *A Study of Oral Reading Miscues That Result in Grammatical Retransformations.* Final Report, June 1969, Project No. 7-E-219, Contract No. oeg-0-8-070219-2806 (010), United States Department of Health, Education, and Welfare, Office of Education.

Shuy, Roger; Wolfram, Walter; and Riley, William. *Field Techniques in an Urban Language Study.* (Washington, D.C.: Center for Applied Linguistics, 1968.)

THE RELATIONSHIP OF
BLACK ENGLISH TO READING:
A Review of Research

JOAN C. BARATZ
Education Study Center
Washington, D.C.

Much has been written concerning the relationship between oral language skills and the acquisition of reading skills. It has been suggested by some that the failure of large numbers of black children to perform at or above national norms on reading achievement tests may be due, at least in part, to the fact that these children do not speak standard English (SE)—the language of instruction and the language of the text—when they first come to school (Baratz and Shuy, 1969). Although there is apparent agreement on the existence of Negro nonstandard English (NNE) and its possible role in reading retardation in black children, there remains a considerable difference of opinion among linguists who have been describing the dialect as to the amount of linguistic interference, the exact source of that interference, and even the amount of bidialectalism among NNE-speaking children. Venezky (1970), who has questioned the effectiveness of vernacular education, and Bailey (1970) have recommended that the problems of NNE-speaking children be dealt with by teaching them to speak SE before teaching them to read. In this way, presumably, there would be no linguistic conflict caused by SE beginning readers, since the NNE-speaking children would already know the language used in them. Wolfram (1970) and Stewart (1970) have questioned the assumption of Bailey and Venezky that children who speak only NNE can be taught SE in six months to a year. In addition, Baratz seriously questions whether the delaying of the teaching of reading to black children would not provoke as great a controversy as early reading instruction using dialect texts would. Earlier efforts to delay reading instruction until eight or nine (when the child's neurological system is further matured) met with considerable rejection by parents in middle-class communities who wanted their children to be taught reading when they entered first grade. Nonetheless, the teach-SE-first alternative deserves to be tested.

Labov (1967) attributes the poor reading performance of many black children to "the ignorance of SE rules" on the part of the black youngsters on the one hand and to "the ignorance of nonstandard English rules on the part of teachers and text-writers" on the other hand. In fact, he feels that "the great differences in the sets of homonyms" in NNE and SE may well result in confusion in every reading assignment" (Melmed, 1970). For this reason, Labov sees the solution to teaching black NNE speakers to read as one of teacher education. That is, teachers must learn the rules of the dialect (especially as they relate to the phonology) so that they will not inadvertently penalize a child for a "reading error" which in fact is merely a NNE pronunciation.

Shuy (1969) takes the position that the best way to deal with the problems of NNE interference in learning to read SE is not only to teach the teachers about the phonology but also to construct special materials that would avoid those areas where there is potential syntactic interference with SE. The difficulty here, as Wolfram (1970) has pointed out, is that it is virtually impossible to write a text if one wishes to avoid all the potential points of syntactic interference. Indeed, the Shuy-Ginn (Project 360) approach (which one might call a "nonlinguistic" alternative in that it consciously attempts to avoid aspects of the child's linguistic competence) has no data to stand on, save the publisher's recommendation. And, given the past performance of such commercial materials, one cannot be optimistic. This "nonlinguistic" idea, however, deserves to be tested; only then—on the basis of, not prior to, results from such tests—should avoidance materials be promoted or rejected.

Baratz (1968) and Stewart (1967, 1969) have called for both teacher training and special materials for teaching NNE-speaking children to read. They have both suggested that, although phonological interference probably does occur, it is not likely to be the primary source of difficulty in reading. Concerning this problem, Stewart (1969) points out that:

> . . . if the differences [between SE and NNE phonology] are regular enough, which they often are, then the Negro dialect speaker may be able to set up his own sound-spelling correspondences between them—ones which will be different from those set up by a speaker of SE, but which will allow effective word identification nevertheless (pp. 177-78).

In fact, a phonics program can be constructed that makes the sound-spelling correspondence between SE orthography and NE phonology explicit for the child.

Baratz (1969a) has stressed the importance of interference on the syntactic level:

> Despite the obvious mismatch of the "teachers' and text writers' " phoneme system and that of the inner city child, the difficulties of the disadvantaged Negro child cannot be simplified solely to the pronunciation and phoneme differences that exist in the two systems. There is an even more serious problem facing the inner city child which concerns his unfamiliarity with the syntax of the classroom texts (p. 202).

Because of the mismatch between the child's syntactic system and that of the SE textbook, because of the psychological consequences of denying the existence and legitimacy of the child's linguistic system, and because of the success of vernacular teaching around the world, Baratz (1969b) has joined Stewart and others in calling for experimentation with reading instruction using texts that employ NNE syntax while preserving SE orthography.

These various discussions concerning the interference of NNE on the acquisition of standard English reading skills have spawned several studies attempting to determine whether there is in fact any interference from NNE on SE reading proficiency and, if so, the nature of that interference.

The first group of such studies was concerned with an analysis of the miscues of black children when reading SE (Goodman, 1968; Weber, 1969). The Goodman studies did not reveal much overt interference from NNE syntax, except when a fluent reader became engrossed in a story. Indeed, on the basis of his data concerning miscues involving dialect, Goodman hypothesized that:

> . . . as a reader with a deviant dialect gains proficiency [in reading], the number of dialect related miscues will increase. The assumption here being that with added comfort and less emphasis of the individual symbols involved, an actual translation process will begin to emerge in which the dialect of the material is translated into the dialect of the reader (p. 43).

Thus Goodman confirmed a tendency which Stewart had noticed years earlier (Stewart, 1964). As useful as Goodman's studies have been in throwing light on the role of dialect differences in the oral performance connected with reading aloud, they leave largely unresolved a fundamental question of dialect interference in reading: Does it affect reading comprehension?

Weber (1969), too, did not find significant interference from NNE on children's reading miscues. However, the very nature of her design and selection of subjects may be responsible for this negative finding. She compared first grade white children from upstate New York with second grade and post-second grade black children from the District of Columbia on a typical first-grade reading passage. She eliminated any subject who made fewer than three, or more than eleven, reading miscues because she did not want "so many [errors] as to render the passage incoherent and thus stifle the young reader's ordinary use of contextual cues for proceeding through the passage, to say nothing of comprehending it." It is necessary, however, to understand that those linguists who were discussing the possible effect of NNE on the ability to read SE texts were concerned with precisely what Miss Weber rules out of consideration from her study, i.e., the effect of a SE text on a young black reader's potential use of ordinary cues (in this case, the grammar of NNE) for proceeding through a written passage, to say nothing of comprehending it! The very difficulty one encounters in locating black children at the first grade level to compare with white children in such tests serves further to underscore this point. In her study, Weber included only black children who seemed to be capable of reading the test passage. As a result, she had to use black children a year older than her white children in order to find a sufficient number of children who could cope with the passage at her criterion level. In fact, Weber's criteria virtually ruled out readers who might have exhibited dialect interference.

In a later study, which is in some respects similar to Weber's, Rystrom (1970) also asserted that the purpose of his research was "to determine the extent to which Negro dialect interferes with the acquisition of reading skills." Yet his entire study displayed an appalling ignorance concerning the very issue which he attempted to elucidate. He showed no evidence of having grasped the essential nature of the difference vs. deficit controversy—a failing which was pointed out by Goodman (1970) in his criticism of Rystrom's research. In addition, Rystrom's handling of NNE (or, rather, what he claimed to represent NNE) showed that he was most unclear as to the difference between phonology, morphology, and syntax—to say nothing of his confusion concerning the nature of dialect and dialect variation in the United States (another point discussed briefly by Goodman in his criticism). At no point did Rystrom actually examine the relationship between dialect differences and reading acquisition. What he did instead was to examine the effect of a hopelessly confused "dialect training course" in which, among other things, the copula form *is* was taught as an example of the "third person marker" (i.e., the drill for third person marking was "This *is* the way we wash our clothes"). Along the same line, one of the most serious products of Rystrom's linguistic naiveté was his apparent belief in a universal "linguistic" reader. Although the series he called "linguistic" was constructed so as to present a consistent sound-spelling correspondence, that correspondence was not consistent with the dialect of the children involved in his study, and therefore could hardly be considered as an appropriate "linguistic reader" for them. In summary, all Rystrom really demonstrated, if indeed he demonstrated anything at all, was the fact that black (and presumably NNE-speaking) first-grade children in rural Georgia do not achieve at the first-grade norm on the SAT—a fact which will come as something less than a revelation to reading specialists who have followed the literature on today's educational crisis.

In another recent dissertation, Melmed (1970) attempted to investigate the relationship between black English phonology and reading interference. He was concerned with examining both expressive and receptive competence in standard English phonology (especially in relation to points of difference from the phonology of black English) and the relationship this competence might have to reading proficiency. His interest in the comprehension of standard English was apparently motivated by the work of Claudia Mitchell (Kernan), who asserted in her dissertation, "It is the unhesitating opinion of this writer that, whatever difficulty some black English speakers exhibit in producing SE variants, there is not a corresponding difficulty in comprehending SE" (Mitchell, 1969). Yet Mitchell-Kernan was primarily concerned with SE/BE syntactic variation in her statement: whereas, Melmed was concerned in his thesis only with phonology. Nonetheless, since Mitchell-Kernan's statement was nothing more than "unhesitating opinion" (with no data on mutual intelligibility presented in her thesis beyond a few sentence repetition tests with older crildren—hardly a test of receptive competence), Melmed did attempt to gather some data concerning mutual intelligibility of SE/NNE phonological variation.

Melmed constructed tests of auditory discrimination, oral and silent reading comprehension, and speech production involving the five phonological differences which Labov (1967) identified as potential sources for interference between the phonologies of SE and NNE. Melmed found that black subjects did significantly poorer than white and other subjects (primarily Mexican-Americans) on the auditory discrimination and oral production tests but did not differ from disadvantaged whites and Mexican-Americans in SE reading competence.

Unfortunately, there is a major difficulty with Melmed's study. The sample studied was exceptional in that all the disadvantaged children—black, white, and Mexican-American—were already reading at or above grade level; thus it was not at all characteristic of the disadvantaged population in regard to reading performance. Melmed (personal communication, February 1971) had indicated that his sample was indeed an atypical third grade class. Thus, Melmed tested a group of disadvantaged children, who he admitted were extraordinary and who had learned to read, and he demonstrated that they had in fact learned to read.

Melmed, however, did call for more research concerning the relationship of syntactic interference and reading, since he only dealt with phonology and since Baratz and Stewart have been stressing that the major source of difficulty may well be with the syntax. Furthermore, Melmed, echoing many before him (Baratz and Baratz, 1968; Baratz and Shuy, 1969; Stewart, 1967, 1969, 1970), suggested that a project should be initiated to see if black children can learn to read if they are first taught in dialect syntax.

Davis, Gladney, and Leaverton (1969) several years ago began preparing materials to test the hypothesis that teaching children to read in the dialect would be helpful in terms of their ultimately learning to read standard English. Unfortunately, due to the small number of subjects, the sparseness of dialect content, and the methodology involved, it is impossible, from their study, to evaluate the effect of dialect readers on learning to read (Leaverton, 1971). Only one class, with thirty-five children, was used. The same teacher instructed the children for two years. This teacher was apparently very gifted, and there is no reason to believe that she could not have taught these children with any type of materials, especially if the Hawthorne Effect were considered. Indeed, the involvement of this teacher was so great that she gave extra after-school attention to some of the poorer-achieving students in the control group—obliging Leaverton to ask her also to give additional special attention to the experimental group. In addition, the subjects in this study were not assigned to the dialect reading group on the basis of their speech patterns, so it is not clear whether all the experimental subjects should have received the dialect materials.

In another study purporting to present data on dialect interference and reading, Fasold (1971), with help from Wolfram, Shuy, and Anisman, gave a NNE version of the Bible passage John 3:16 (For God so loved the world . . .) to six black NNE-speaking teenagers and asked them to read it twice—once as it stood and a second time supplying every seventh word which had been deleted. They found that the students hesitated or supplied the SE equivalent approximately 24 percent of the time. However, their data were very confused; they said, for example, that there were 34 chances for the six students to deal with the θ copula—yet, this comes out to $5\frac{3}{5}$ chances per student! And their analysis of the seventh word cloze technique was not presented. In addition, they stated that their questions concerning whether the dialect version was preferred were not well understood. Nonetheless, these researchers concluded that the boys would prefer at least Biblical materials that were not written in NNE.

Baratz (1970b) in a study with 481 black first and second graders in the District of Columbia parochial schools discovered a significant correlation between learning to read and facility with SE. She gave the children a sentence repetition task involving SE and NNE and, on the basis of their performance, classified them as monodialectal in NNE or SE, or bidialectal. All students were also given the Lyons and Carnahan, New Developmental Reading Tests—Bond-Balow-Hoyt, Lower Primary Reading, Form L-II. A comparison of reading comprehension of the monodialectal NNE children in relation to the SE and bidialectal children revealed a significant difference (beyond .001) in favor of the SE group. These data suggest that monodialectal NNE speaking children are not learning to read with traditional materials as well as are SE speaking children.

In summary, a review of the data concerning dialect interference and learning to read reveals that there are still no real tests of the alternatives discussed earlier, and the extant data are ambiguous at best and do not deal with using dialect as a process in reading instruction. There is, however, a noticeable backing away from testing the dialect-text alternative because of its controversy.

But what really are the issues involved in the backing away, since there was no data to discount the effectiveness of the dialect-text alternative? Although there is virtually complete agreement among the researchers that NNE does exist, there is also a strong feeling that the major difficulty with using dialect texts, and therefore the reason they should not be used, is that black parents and teachers reject these texts. It is, however, primarily the Johnny-come-latelys to the dialect research issue who are intimidated by the rejection of the dialect by blacks. Indeed, if in the early 1960s deference to the rejection of discussions of NNE had been heeded by Dillard, Stewart, Johnson, and others, there would be no acceptance today of the existence of NNE and therefore no discussion of its possible relationship to reading.

That blacks reject the dialect and dialect readers is a fact, a fact that has been documented in several places (Baratz, 1970 a and b; Stewart, 1970; and Wolfram, 1970). That that rejection may be understood from an historical perspective is also clear. Nonetheless, that rejection must be met head on and dealt with in the same manner that the earlier objections to the mere mention of the existence of NNE were overcome—at least superficially.

It should be clear from the foregoing review, however, that there is still a crying need for adequate research on the question of dialect interference in the acquisition of reading skills. Consequently, the possibility that dialect readers might prove useful in the process of learning to read must be dealt with as an empirical question, involving their effect on children who otherwise are not learning to read. This possibility cannot be rejected by mere reason of the fact that some children who seem to speak the dialect have learned to read anyway, since there remain many, many more who speak the dialect and who have not learned to read by traditional methods. Nor can the possibility of using dialect readers as part of the process of beginning reading be rejected on the basis of the known negative attitudes of black parents, teachers, and community spokesmen to the pedagogical use of the dialect in print. While it is true that they may say of NNE "That's just slave-talk" or "That ain't no real language" or "That's broken English'" or "It's bad language" or "It'll hold the children back," such statements are just as much a manifestation of ignorance of misunderstanding as similar statements about any other form of human language would be. Such statements cannot be accepted by educators as the final answer on the matter, because the role of education is to inform others and to act on knowledge, rather than to perpetuate misunderstanding and act on mere folk beliefs. Thus, it is no less important for educators to stand up to black parents and spokesmen who say ignorant things about black language than it is to confront white parents and spokesmen who say ignorant things about black children.

The school use of dialect readers may not, in the early 1970s, be "an idea whose time has come," but, as Carrington (1971) has said in support of dialect readers for St. Lucia (but not yet for Jamaica), when the educational situation becomes desperate enough and the consumer-public frantic enough about the literacy problem, dialect readers will be an idea whose time has come.

References

Bailey, Beryl Loftman. "Some Arguments Against the Use of Dialect Readers in the Teaching of Initial Reading," *Florida FL Reporter*, 8:1-2 (Spring/Fall 1970), 8, 47.

Baratz, Joan C. "Beginning Readers for Speakers of Divergent Dialects," *Reading Goals for the Disadvantaged*, J. Allen Figurel, Ed. Newark, Delaware: International Reading Association, 1970a, 77-83.

Baratz, Joan C. "Linguistic and Cultural Factors in Teaching Reading to Ghetto Children," *Elementary English,* 46 (February 1969a), 199-203.

Baratz, Joan C. *Relationship of Negro Non-standard English Dialect Speech to Reading Achievement,* unpublished paper, Education Study Center, 1970b.

Baratz, Joan C. "Teaching Reading in an Urban Negro School System," *Teaching Black Children to Read,* Joan Baratz and Roger Shuy, Eds. (Washington, D.C.: Center for Applied Linguistics, 1969b), 92-115.

Baratz, Joan, and Shuy, Roger, Eds. *Teaching Black Children to Read.* (Washington, D.C.: Center for Applied Linguistics, 1969b).

Baratz, Stephen S., and Baratz, Joan C. "Negro Ghetto Children and Urban Education: A Cultural Solution," *Bulletin of Minnesota Council for Social Studies* (Fall 1968), 1-3. Reprinted in *Social Education,* 33 (1969), 401-04.

Carrington, Lawrence D. *Language Culture and Education: A Symposium.* (Washington, D.C.: American Orthopsychiatric Association, March 1971.)

Davis, Olga; Gladney, Mildred R.; and Leaverton, Lloyd. Teachers Manual of *The Psycholinguistics Reading Series, A Bidialectal Approach.* Chicago: Board of Education, 1967.

Fasold, Ralph W. *Report on the Use of a Dialect Bible Translation with* YDI *Teenagers,* unpublished paper, Center for Applied Linguistics, 1971.

Frazier, Alexander, Ed. *New Directions in Elementary English.* (Champaign, Illinois: National Council of Teachers of English, 1967.)

Goodman, Kenneth. "Dialect Rejection and Reading: A Response," *Reading Research Quarterly,* 4 (1970), 600-03.

Goodman, Kenneth. *Study of Children's Behavior While Reading Orally.* Final Report Project S425, Contract #OE-6-10-136, 1968.

Labov, William. "Some Sources of Reading Problems for Negro Speakers of Nonstandard English," *New Directions in Elementary English,* Alexander Frazier, Ed. (Champaign, Illinois: National Council of Teachers of English, 1967), 140-167.

Leaverton, Lloyd. "Dialect Readers—Rationale, Use and Value," International Reading Association Preconvention Institute VIII, Language Development and Reading, 1971.

Melmed, Paul Jay. *Black English Phonology: The Question of Reading Interference,* unpublished doctoral dissertation, University of California, Berkeley, 1970.

Mitchell, Claudia. *Language Behavior in a Black Urban Community,* unpublished doctoral dissertation, University of California, Berkeley, 1969.

Rystrom, Richard. "Dialect Training and Reading: A Further Look," *Reading Research Quarterly,* 4 (1970), 581-600.

Shuy, Roger W. "A Linguistic Background for Developing Beginning Reading Materials for Black Children," *Teaching Black Children to Read,* Joan Baratz and Roger Shuy, Eds., 17-137. (Washington, D.C.: Center for Applied Linguistics, 1969.)

Shuy, Roger W., Ed. *Social Dialects and Language Learning.* (Champaign, Illinois: National Council of Teachers of English, 1964.)

Stewart, William A. "Current Issues in the Use of Negro Dialect in Beginning Reading Texts," *Florida FL Reporter,* 8:1-2 (Spring/Fall 1970), 3-7, 46.

Stewart, William A. *Language and Communication Problems in Southern Appalachia.* Washington, D.C.: Center for Applied Linguistics, 1967.

Stewart, William A. "On the Use of Negro Dialect in the Teaching of Reading," *Teaching Black Children to Read,* Joan Baratz and Roger Shuy, Eds., 156-219. Washington, D.C.: Center for Applied Linguistics, 1969.

Stewart, William A. "Urban Negro Speech: Sociolinguistic Factors Affecting English Teaching," *Social Dialects and Language Learning,* Roger Shuy, Ed., 10-18. Champaign, Illinois: National Council of Teachers of English, 1964.

Venezky, Richard L. "Nonstandard Language and Reading," *Elementary English*, 47 (1970), 334-45.

Weber, Rose-Marie. "Comparing the Oral Reading of Children Who Speak Different Varieties of English," unpublished paper, n.d.

Wolfram, Walt. "Sociolinguistic Alternatives in Teaching Reading to Nonstandard Speakers," *Reading Research Quarterly*, 6 (Fall 1970), 9-33; also reprinted in *Florida FL Reporter*, 8 (Spring/Fall 1970), 16-23, 48.

DIALECTAL READERS:
Rationale, Use, and Value*

LLOYD LEAVERTON
Chicago, Illinois, Board of Education

Since the early 1960s, a few educators, psychologists, and linguists have been considering the possible advantages and disadvantages of utilizing dialectal reading material in primary reading programs (Baratz and Shuy, 1969; Goodman, 1965; Stewart, 1967).

Although considerable attention has been given to nonstandard speech patterns as they may facilitate or hinder progress in the beginning reading situation, no direct experimental evidence has been reported in the literature with respect to the effectiveness of dialectal reading materials as a basal reading program.

The reason for the lack of experimental evidence in this crucial area can partially be explained by considering the following two obstacles encountered in conducting research using reading materials phrased in the nonstandard speech patterns corresponding to the child's oral speech.

The first, and possibly most crucial obstacle, is the difficulty encountered in developing an appropriate model and instructional material through which objective data can be obtained. For example, in testing the effectiveness of dialectal reading materials for beginning reading instruction, who can you use for a control group? If children in the experimental group are given stories which contain sentences such as, "My daddy strong," "My mama pretty," "My grandmama nice," "My cousin mean," they will, after a time, learn the words daddy, mama, grandmama,

* The research described in this paper was cooperatively supported by the Gifted Program Development Section, Department for Exceptional Children, State of Illinois, and the Chicago Board of Education.

cousin, strong, pretty, nice, and mean. If, on the other hand, a basal reading series such as "Dick and Jane" is used for the control group, these children will learn the words Dick, Jane, and Spot. Few meaningful comparisons can be made between the groups. Similarly, if a reading program is used for the control group that places heavy emphasis on phonics, the same problem will be encountered. The control group will have learned more phonics than the experimental group, but just exactly what effect this will have on his ultimate reading ability will not be known.

Also, the standardized tests available to measure progress in primary reading are based on words contained in the most commonly used basal readers. Words needed to develop reading materials utilizing the child's actual speech frequently do not appear in the standardized tests. Hence, these tests would not give a clear measure of the actual achievement of the group using the dialect reading materials.

A second obstacle encountered in conducting research to test the effectiveness of dialect readers is that of developing materials that are acceptable to the school. Because of the stigma frequently attached to the nonstandard speech patterns, it is often difficult to obtain permission to test the materials. It is sometimes difficult to communicate to school personnel that the objective of dialect reading material is not to reinforce the nonstandard aspects of the child's oral speech but instead to employ the child's established speech as a means to help him recognize the relationship between oral language and reading. Stewart (1971) gives an excellent account of some of the resistance that is met when dialect reading materials are introduced in public school systems.

The time involved in conducting an adequate study is also a consideration. To control the experimental variables on a day-to-day basis is both time consuming and exacting. Another time factor involved concerns the length of time needed to conduct the study. It is the writer's opinion, based on his research in this area, that a study lasting a minimum of two years is essential to adequately test the overall effectiveness of dialect readers as a means of teaching beginning reading.

A research model was developed, as part of the writer's unpublished doctoral dissertation, that avoids some of the problems described in the foregoing. Reading materials were also developed based on criteria established by the model.

The research findings resulting from use of the model and materials will be described in this paper.

Theoretical rationale of model used in study

The theoretical rationale of the study is based on the following conditions that are felt to be crucial to the learning process involved in beginning reading.

The first condition is based on the premise that learning to read will be facilitated in direct proportion to the extent that the child can be helped to perceive the close relationship between his spoken language and the written language of the beginning reading materials. When applied to the area of beginning reading, this concept logically suggests utilization of the established speech patterns of the child in the beginning reading materials.

The second condition or premise underlying the theoretical rationale of the model is that at no time should the children be given the impression that the speech forms used in their oral speech are inferior forms of communication.

To render both of the foregoing conditions operational in the model, the *everyday talk* and *school talk* concept was employed. This concept helps the child to distinguish between his familiar oral language patterns and those of the standard dialect without designating one as inferior or superior. Since the child feels most comfortable in using the everyday talk patterns that are familiar to him, the initial emphasis was placed on having the child make the transition from the familiar everyday talk form to the unfamiliar school talk form. Those of us working on the project found that the children readily learned and enjoyed using the idea that the same communication can be stated in more than one way.

The decision to utilize nonstandard speech patterns in the beginning reading situation raised a question as to what aspect of the nonstandard dialect should be emphasized in the materials. In listening to our children, we observed differences in vocabulary, pronunciation, and grammatical form. In considering these differences, we decided to focus only on the difference between the standard and the nonstandard that existed in the area of verb usage. The reasoning for this decision was that even if a standard pronunciation system could be identified and defended, it would not be pedagogically feasible to focus on this aspect of the standard dialect with primary grade children. Also, even if it were possible and feasible to identify and teach a standard pronunciation to our primary children, it seemed to us that there is far more tolerance in our society toward regional variations in pronunciation than toward differences in verb usage.

The decision to focus on verbs as the only distinguishing variable between the nonstandard and standard was also influenced by the fact that in many cases the transition from the nonstandard to the standard pattern could be made by adding to the nonstandard pattern.

Considerable research has been conducted with respect to the conditions in which prior learning interferes with the learning and recall of the new material. Hence, whenever possible, efforts were made to make the distinguishing variable between everyday talk and school talk one in which the transition from everyday talk to school talk could be made by adding to the everyday talk form.

Questions to be investigated

The study was conducted to obtain information with respect to two questions:

1. Will learning to read be facilitated for children whose dialect differs from the standard dialect if the primary reading material is phrased in the actual word patterns and grammatical structure used by the children in their oral speech?

2. Will learning the same story rephrased in speech patterns corresponding to standard English usage be facilitated if the children first learn to read the story phrased in the word patterns and grammatical structure corresponding to their oral speech (Leaverton, 1965)?

Development of experimental materials

To obtain information with respect to the two research questions, it was necessary to develop companion everyday talk and school talk stories. In accordance with the rationale of the study, the school talk stories would need to be the same as the everyday talk stories with the exception that the verb form would be changed to correspond to the standard English usage.

Ideas with respect to content and speech patterns needed to develop the everyday talk stories were obtained from tape recordings of conversations with several groups of kindergarten, first, second, and third grade children attending several inner-city schools in Chicago.

The experimental everyday talk stories were developed, focusing on the particular verb forms that were found to appear frequently in the nonstandard form in the child's informal conversation.

The companion school talk stories were written, utilizing the same sentences in every respect except the verb form, which was changed to correspond to the standard English usage.

The experimental treatments were divided into seven units. The focus of each unit was placed on a particular verb form as follows (Davis, Gladney, and Leaverton, 1968):

	EVERYDAY TALK	SCHOOL TALK
Unit 1	Employs the verb *got*	Introduces the verb *have*
Unit 2	Absence of *is* and *are*	Introduces *is* and *are*
Unit 3	Absence of third person singular ending *-s*	Introduces the verb ending *-s*
Unit 4	Absence of *-ed* ending	Introduces *-ed* ending

EVERYDAY TALK	SCHOOL TALK
Unit 5 Employs use of *do*	Introduces *does*
Unit 6 Employs use of *be* in place of *am, is,* and *are*	Introduces *am, is,* and *are* in place of *be*
Unit 7 Employs *he be, we be,* and *they be*	Introduces standard forms *he is, we are,* and *they are* in place of *he be, we be,* and *they be*

Grouping of students

To insure that groups were matched as closely as possible, the Wechsler Intelligence Scale for Children was given to each of the 37 pupils in the experimental classroom. The students were representative of the school population as a whole with respect to ability. Scores were separated with respect to sex and ranked from highest to lowest total IQ. Proceeding from highest to lowest, each student was alternately assigned to one of two groups. For example, the highest ranking student was assigned to Group 1, the second ranking student to Group 2, the next to Group 1, etc. This same procedure was used for both male and female students. After all assignments had been made, the experimental group was chosen by tossing a coin.

Presentation of treatments

Group 1 (the experimental group) was given the everyday talk version of each story, and Group 2 (the control group) was given the school talk version of the same story. When, in the judgment of the teacher, half of the experimental group had reasonably mastered the everyday talk story, word recognition and phrase recognition tests were administered to both groups.

This measure was designed to test the first question, i.e., "Will the children learn to read the everyday talk stories quicker than the school talk stories?"

When, in the judgment of the teacher, approximately half of the experimental group were able to read the school talk story orally without mistakes, both groups were given word recognition and phrase recognition tests. This measure was designed to test the second question, i.e., "Will learning to read the everyday talk story facilitate the learning of the school talk story?"

This sequence was followed for each story included in the unit. Figure 1 illustrates the administration of the word recognition and phrase recognition tests.

Figure 1. Sequence of Administration of Treatments

	Story I		Story II		Story III		Story IV	
Group 1	ET	ST	ET	ST	ET	ST	ET	ST
Group 2	ST	ST	ST	ST	ST	ST	ST	ST
	T_1	T_2	T_1	T_2	T_1	T_2	T_1	T_2

ET — Represents the *everyday talk* story.

ST — Represents the *school talk* story.

T_1 — Represents the tests administered relative to Question 1.

T_2 — Represents the tests administered relative to Question 2.

Methods of evaluation

Word recognition and phrase recognition tests. Word recognition and phrase recognition tests were administered as described in the foregoing section.

Oral Review Tests. Oral review tests were administered at the completion of each unit. These tests utilized the same vocabulary included in the unit. The words and phrases, however, were rearranged to alter the content and meaning of each story. For example, the sentence "My Daddy is strong" might be changed in the oral review to "My Daddy is smart." The groups were compared with respect to 1) total mean errors (scoring adopted from Gray's Oral Reading Test), 2) errors on verb form only, and 3) time required to read the story.

Figure 2. Design Used in Administering the Oral Review Tests

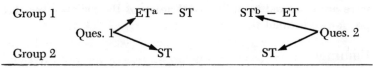

a — ET represents one-half of Group 1 who
   read the ET review story first.
b — ST represents one-half of Group 2 who
   read the ST review story first.

Figure 2 shows the design used in administering the oral review tests. This design was used because in evaluating the
second question, a practice effect would have been present if all
of Group 1 read the everyday talk first. This practice effect would
result from the fact that in order to facilitate the administration
of the oral review tests, the child was prompted after six seconds
if he did not know a word. The following everyday talk story
will serve as an example:

Stop That!

When I be talking my teacher say, "Stop that!"
When I be running my teacher say, "Stop that!"
When I be fighting my teacher say, "Stop that!"
No talking!
No running!
No fighting!
What a school!

Note that the only difference between the everyday talk and
school talk is with respect to the verb be/am, and say/says.
Hence, if in reading the everyday talk oral review story the child
had been prompted on *teacher, stop that, when,* or *talking, running,* and *fighting,* he would have received practice effect on
these words as they also appear in the school talk story.

Retention Tests. Approximately four to six months after both groups completed a unit, word recognition and oral review tests were administered to evaluate retention of the material that was previously learned.

Findings

Data were obtained and categorized with respect to the following variables:

1. Mean rank* and U score values with respect to the combined errors on word recognition and phrase recognition tests relative to both research questions being investigated. Values were obtained individually for each unit in the experimental materials.

2. "t" ratios were calculated for each unit comparing mean errors made by each group on the oral review tests.

3. "t" ratios calculated for each unit comparing mean errors made by each group on the oral review *retention* tests.

4. Mean rank and U score values with respect to errors only on the verb form on the oral review tests.

5. "t" ratios calculated from comparison of mean time taken to read the oral review and oral review retention tests relative to both questions being investigated.**

It was apparent from inspecting the mean errors and time taken to read the story on the oral review and retention tests that there was a definite trend in favor of the experimental group. To determine how often this trend could occur by chance, a chi square was calculated on the three variables evaluated by the oral review and oral review retention tests, i.e., 1) total mean errors, 2) mean errors on verb form, and 3) time taken to read story.

---

* The scores for both groups were combined and ranked in order of increasing size. The sum of the ranks for the scores in each group (R_1 and R_2) was then obtained, and a mean for each sum was calculated.

** Detailed analysis of the findings from the comparisons cited above will be discussed in the author's forthcoming doctoral dissertation. Hence, only a summary of the findings will be discussed at this time.

Tables 1, 2, and 3 show the results of this analysis.

TABLE 1. X^2 calculated from frequency that group mean for Group 1 was lower than that of Group 2 with respect to mean errors on the oral review and oral retention tests.

	Question 1[a]		Question 2	
	Group 1	Group 2	Group 1	Group 2
Observed	10	0	9	1
Expected	5	5	5	5

DF = 1   DF = 1
X^2 = 8.10 X^2 = 4.90
P   =   .01   P   =   .05

[a] Yates correction was used in calculating the X^2.

TABLE 2. X^2 calculated from frequency of occasions in which mean rank of Group 1 was lower than Group 2 with respect to errors only on the verb form on the oral review test and oral review retention test.

	Question 1[a]		Question 2	
	Group 1	Group 2	Group 1	Group 2
Observed	8	1	7	3
Expected	4.5	4.5	5	5

DF = 1   DF = 1
X^2 = 4 X^2 =   .90
P   =   .05   P   = NS

[a] Yates correction was used in calculating the X^2.

TABLE 3. X^2 calculated from frequency that group mean for Group 1 was lower than that of Group 2 with respect to time taken to read the oral review and oral review retention tests.

	Question 1[a]		Question 2	
	Group 1	Group 2	Group 1	Group 2
Observed	9	1	9	1
Expected	5	5	5	5

DF = 1   DF = 1
X^2 = 4.9 X^2 = 4.9
P = .05   P = .05

[a] Yates correction was used in calculating the X^2.

Implications for future research

As can be noted from the foregoing tables, the findings are positive. However, because of the small number involved in this study, the results need to be replicated with a larger group. A study is in progress whereby forty classrooms of children who started with the experimental materials in September, 1969 will be compared with children in several other special reading programs for inner-city children in Chicago (Leaverton, 1971).

During the 1971–1972 school year, these children will receive the standardized reading test given to third-grade children in Chicago on a citywide basis. In addition, results will be available from all other tests given to the children since they entered school, i.e., IQ, reading readiness, etc. This will allow comparison of the reading achievement of the children in each program with respect to several variables.

The data from the present study strongly suggests that dialect readers are especially effective with boys who scored in the lowest quartile on the reading readiness test administered at the beginning of first grade. Therefore, special attention will be given in the study under progress to determine to what extent and under what conditions this finding is verified.

Value

Possibly the most significant value of the language arts instructional model used in our research lies in the influence it has on the attitude and behavior of the teacher toward the children's oral speech. The traditional approaches to reading and oral language programs for the most part have not considered the possible negative effect that constant criticism of the child's nonstandard speech patterns can have on the interaction between teacher and child and on the ultimate learning experience. It is possible that the difficulty that many of our children have in learning to read results in their resistance to a learning situation that belittles the speech patterns they have learned from their parents and community.

In using the model just described, the teacher is at no time required to criticize the oral speech of the children while they are beginning to read or during oral language arts activities. On the contrary, the model encourages the teacher to respect and accept the children's dialect, and at the same time provide a framework to help the children learn to read and gradually and systematically to use standard English in their oral language activities. Hence, the model functions as a training program for the teacher as well as an instructional program for the children.

References

Baratz, Joan, and Shuy, Roger, Editors. *Teaching Black Children to Read.* (Washington, D.C.: Center for Applied Linguistics, 1969.)

Davis, Olga; Gladney, Mildred; and Leaverton, Lloyd. *The Psycholinguistics Reading Series* (A bi-dialectal approach), Chicago Board of Education, 1968.

Goodman, K. S., "Dialect Barriers to Reading Comprehension," *Elementary English,* December 1965.

Leaverton, Lloyd. "An Experimental Language Arts Program for Potentially Gifted Culturally Disadvantaged Primary Children," 1965 proposal to superintendent of public instruction, state of Illinois.

Leaverton, Lloyd. "Follow-up Three Years Later of 1,400 Children Who Learned to Read Using the Psycholinguistics Reading Series," 1971 proposal to superintendent of public instruction, state of Illinois.

Stewart, William A. "Language and Communication Problems in Southern Appalachia," (Washington, D.C.: Center for Applied Linguistics, 1967.)

Stewart, William A. "Current Issues in the Use of Negro Dialect in Beginning Reading Texts," *Florida FL Reporter*, 8 (Spring/Fall 1970), 3-7, 46.

CULTURALLY DIVERGENT CHILDREN AND CREATIVE LANGUAGE ACTIVITIES

A. Barbara Pilon
Worcester State College

Tony Cavin, who wrote a book of poetry called *The Bright Red Porcupine* (1969), included in his collection a poem which seems to be a most appropriate one to use at the beginning of a paper which is concerned with language and, thus, reading growth and development. Here is Tony's poem:

> I was once
> At the bottom of a lake
> In the mud
> With the fish
> Talking and playing
> And I noticed something:
> The fish did not swim in straight lines.
> Why aren't people like that?

(Used by permission of Harlin Quist, Inc.)

A plea for encouraging and reinforcing language diversity

Our English language is a rich language because as a people we have not been afraid to take words we liked from any language. We have become language rich because we have been interested in diversity and divergency. We have tended to include, invent, and expand word meanings rather than exclude and restrict our nation's word bank. Language diversity and divergency characteristics as seen in the writings of our greatest novelists, playwrights, and poets have always connoted positive feelings. They have brought to mind such discriptors as

127

original, creative, and *fluent.* Thus, the term, *the divergent speaker,* which Goodman (1969) uses is a well-chosen, realistic, and positive term. Goodman employs this term when he speaks about children who, in some instances, use dialects and syntactical patterns that differ from the language of a speaker who customarily uses what is referred to as the mainstream language. Other terms which have been used synonymously with the divergent speaker include such labels as *substandard* and *nonstandard.* These are terms that frequently imply negative attitudes. Unfortunately, a person rarely thinks of positive language attributes when the word nonstandard is used to describe his or someone else's manner of communicating.

One question that should be posed is: Does any child learn a nonstandard language? Or does a child simply learn what he is exposed to and reinforced for?

Another question that should be raised is: Is the overall language of culturally divergent children impoverished? Do they use language that is rich in imagery; do they have thoughts well worth expressing; do they express themselves creatively and imaginatively?

Torrance in "Creative Positives of Disadvantaged Children and Youth" (1969) states that these children's language is rich in imagery. Riessman (1966) in his booklet, *Helping the Disadvantaged Pupil to Learn More Easily,* includes a dictionary of words compiled by Tony Romeo. This section of words and their definitions as they are used by "disadvantaged" students is called, "The Other Language." Some of the words which have become very much a part of "in" talk are *bread, cool it, cop out,* and *pad.*

There are also many other expressions which have come from the language of the divergent speaker and which all of us know and use and like: *heavy, rap, right on, tough, out of sight, all together, bad, mean, groovy, jazz, jive, main man,* and *boss,* just to name several. The take-over of these words by many middle- and upper-class Americans proves that the child who may come from an inner-city area is very creative in his language. If these expressions are so "in," why is inner-city language as a whole considered so "out"? Teachers should make sure that their students realize where these expressions are coming from and concentrate on the "in" expressions at least as much as the sometimes "out" ones.

For those who may feel that children from inner-city areas are suffering from communication deficiencies, the books listed below should be of special interest. They are written by "disadvantaged" young people, but both inner-city and outer-city students as well as their teachers should have a chance to be exposed to these works. (A group discussion as to whether these youngsters' language is disadvantaged might follow the reading.)

Here I Am! An Anthology of Poems Written by Young People in Some of America's Minority Groups, edited by Virginia Olsen Baron, illustrated by Emily Arnold McCully. (New York: E. P. Dutton, 1969.)

An Empty Spoon by Sunny Decker. (New York: Scholastic Book Services, 1969.)

What Is a City? Young People Reply, compiled by Diane Farrell and Ruth M. Hayes. (Boston: Boston Public Library, 1969.)

Black Means by Barney Grossman with Gladys Groom and the pupils of P.S. 150, The Bronx, New York, illustrated by Charles Bible. (New York: Hill and Wang, 1970.)

Poems by Kali by Kali Grosvenor. (New York: Doubleday, 1970.)

The Way It Is, edited by John Holland. (New York: Harcourt, Brace and World, 1969.)

City Talk, compiled by Lee Bennett Hopkins. (New York: Alfred A. Knopf, 1970.)

The Voice of the Children, collected by June Jordan and Terri Bush. (New York: Holt, Rinehart and Winston, 1970.)

The Me Nobody Knows: Children's Voices from the Ghetto, edited by Stephen M. Joseph. (New York: Avon, 1969.)

I Heard a Scream in the Street, selected by Nancy Larrick. (Philadelphia: J. B. Lippincott, 1970.)

Can't You Hear Me Talking to You? by Carolyn Mirthes and the children of P.S. 15. (New York: Bantam, 1971.)

Stevie by John Steptoe. (New York: Harper and Row, 1969.)

Train Ride by John Steptoe. (New York: Harper and Row, 1971.)

Uptown by John Steptoe. (New York: Harper and Row, 1970.)

The Other City by Ray Vogel. (New York: David White, 1969.)

By reading books of the kind listed and by making them accessible to students, teachers can show children that they really are appreciative of dialectical differences. They are not just paying lip service to an objective they say is desirable, but they are translating their verbal homage into believable actions. Children should be exposed to records such as, "The Year of Roosevelt Franklin, Gordon's Friend from Sesame Street" and "He Ain't Heavy . . . He's My Brother."

By reading and by having available books such as John Shearer's *I Wish I Had an Afro* (Cowles, 1970); Theodore Taylor's *The Cay* (Doubleday, 1969); or Glen Rounds' *The Boll Weevil* (Golden Gate Junior Books, 1967), children will begin believing that divergencies in dialects are fine—a conviction that is basic for them if their language and reading abilities are to blossom and grow. If they feel that their speech is valued and most acceptable, they will not be afraid of being penalized for expressing themselves. This whole discussion, of course, infers that a reading teacher is a *reading* teacher! Children from all schools should be introduced to authors such as Gwendolyn Brooks, Paul Dunbar, and Langston Hughes. Surely, no one would look down in a condescending way upon Hughes' poem, "Mother to Son" which appears in so many anthologies. One of the most memorable lines in this poem is, "Life for me ain't been no crystal stair."

In a recent musical, *Joy,* put together by two American black artists, Jean Pace and Oscar Brown, Jr., and by a Brazilian, Luiz Henrique, there is a lyrical love song by Brown called "Much As I Love You." One of the lines in the song includes these words,

"No man ever *love* a woman much as I love you." (Italics are
those of the writer of this paper.) The record from this play is
available from RCA (LSO-1166). Older students can be asked to
listen to this song and comment on what would happen to the
meaning of the line if the standard English past inflectional
marker *-ed* were added to the word *love*. The line would lose its
perfectly expressed idea of the timelessness of the speaker's love.
Its poetic quality would disappear. The nonstandard and creative
use of language in this line enhances and underscores the main
idea Oscar Brown wanted to convey.

If teachers are to succeed in helping children appreciate language that is well expressed, and if they are to succeed in helping
children comprehend language, then they, as teachers, must
expand their own word meanings as well as their students'. A
fine approach that some middle- and upper-class teachers are
using in their classrooms is one in which the teachers ask the
children if any of them would like to be involved in helping each
other (pupils and teachers) expand one another's vocabularies.
This is done by the children and teachers working together and
preparing a dictionary which incorporates divergent and convergent words and their meanings. In such a situation, both the
teachers and the children are learning together on an equal basis.

Teachers who are aware of the differences in meaning which
various words may have for some children who come from inner-
city areas might not choose to introduce a sentence such as the
one found in a basal reading textbook. Supposedly the purpose
of the sentence was to help children comprehend the primary
meaning of the word *chicken*. The sentence went something like
this: "A bird that lives on a farm is a chicken." Some children
might think that it was very humorous for their teacher not to
"get" the double meaning for this sentence. For those children
who possess nonstandard or nonprimary word meanings for some
of the words used in this sentence, there could be a serious comprehension problem. Thus, children must have teachers who
are cognizant of the possibility of the misconceptions such sentences can produce in youngsters' minds.

The reason people do or do not understand various symbolic messages has to do with the sparseness or the wealth of the language input they have been fed. The more word meaning input and the more mastery of word meaning input one has, the more understanding and appreciation of language there can be.

Riessman in *Helping the Disadvantaged Pupil to Learn More Easily* (1966) includes an excellent description of how one teacher who used Langston Hughes' poem, "Motto," taught children the importance of "digging all jive." The teacher presented the lesson in a very creative way and motivated children to expand their word meanings. The last sentence of the excerpt states, "For the student who has read Shakespeare but has not read Langston Hughes, for example, is also disadvantaged." The same comment could be made about teachers. For us to stay alive, we must be able to "dig all jive." For if we do not, we can neither communicate with nor understand each other.

A philosophical point of view

From what has been stated, some persons may infer that children who are culturally divergent in some aspects need no help in their language. This interpretation certainly is not intended. All children should have their language experiences enriched and broadened—this is one of the goals of every language arts teacher. Those expressions that may hurt children if they use them in certain settings must be identified, and effective teaching methods must be set up so that alternate patterns of expression can become so familiar to the children and sound so right to them that they actually will use the expressions as substitute means of communicating.

It has been stated (Fasold and Shuy, 1970) that "most linguists will agree that a speaker of any language will make linguistic adjustments to specific social situations." It might be pointed out that it is critical for a person in "specific-social situations" to be able to make adequate and sufficient adjustments to the situations. These adjustments probably can occur if a person has used the contextually acceptable verbal alternates orally enough that they are raised high in his habit-family hierarchy. Then they can be used automatically when they are appropriate. This means that a person should be able to use oral language alternatives that will not penalize him, even when he is in an oral social situation that might be stressful to him. What we as educators need to do is to have children become masters of their language variables. They need to be able to use the relevant variable at the relevant time.

Labov (1970) says:

> *Overt* correction applied in the schoolroom is *useful* to the student in that it makes him aware of the distance between his speech and the standard language—in grammar and pronunciation. This correction cannot in itself teach him a new Type I rule; it most often gives him a variable Type III rule which *he will use* in formal situations (p. 36).

[Italics are those of the writer of this paper.]

However, thought needs to be given to the way in which overt corrections can be made. It is possible that a teacher may correct his students in such a way that it causes them to become negative and hostile to everything the teacher stands for. It is also possible that such overt correction does not teach these children anything positive or constructive which will enable them to change their language. They may just feel that their language is "wrong." A quotation from Aristotle seems relevant at this time. He said, "He who knows what justice is, is not immediately just."

Time magazine has on different occasions taken great delight in sharing with its readers some completely inappropriate remarks made to members of Britain's royal family. The people who committed the verbal gaucheries certainly had heard and been exposed to more fitting remarks to make on such occasions. But the standard responses that should have been used obviously were not the ones that the unwitting verbal blunderers were accustomed to using habitually. And so, in each case, a grand *faux pas* too flagrant to overlook was the result.

If teachers are to help children who may commonly be accustomed to expressing themselves in ways that can hinder them in their language arts progress, it is imperative that the teachers diagnose *each* child's difficulties. They should group the children according to their problems and concentrate first on those difficulties that may interfere most with the children's ability to attain their academic and self-fulfillment peak—for the two usually are bound together inextricably. That is, the self-concept bone is most often connected to the achievement bone.

There are many books, such as *Teaching Black Children to Read* (Baratz and Shuy, 1970) and *Teaching Standard English in the Inner City* (Fasold and Shuy, 1970), which describe some specific speech divergencies that can cause black children to experience difficulties with oral expressions, reading, writing, and spelling.

In an article entitled "Blacks," Johnson (1970) makes an extremely important statement:

> Children should have a reading program that takes account of the phonological and structural difference between their nonstandard dialect and standard English, in particular those that produce interference. This means that the reading program must be custom-made for disadvantaged black children, and it must be coordinated and *conducted concurrently with the language program* (35-36).
>
> [Italics are those of the author of this paper.]

Smith, Goodman, and Meredith (1970) give a very pointed illustration of what happens if teachers do not coordinate their reading programs with their language programs:

> A group of second-graders were reading in round-robin fashion. It was Jim's turn. "There was a lot of goats," he read. "There was black goats and white goats."
>
> His teacher smiled encouragingly. "Would you repeat that, please, Jim," she said.

Somewhat puzzled, Jim reread: "There was a lot of goats. There was black goats and white goats."

Still smiling, his teacher stepped to the board. In excellent manuscript she wrote two words. "Do you see a difference in these words?" she said.

"Yes, they have different endings," said Jim.

"Can you read these words?" the teacher asked.

"Was, were," Jim read.

"Good," said his teacher.

"This is was, and this is were. Now read again what you just read from the book."

"There was a lot of . . ." Jim began.

"No, no!" his teacher said with some annoyance. "It's were. 'There were a lot of goats.' Now, please reread."

"There were a lot of goats. There was black goats and . . ." (pp. 61-62).

[Taken from Kenneth S. Goodman, "The Linguistics of Reading," *Elementary School Journal*, 64 (April 1964).]

Unfortunately, too many reading lessons of the kind described in this book are taking place in our country. The approach recommended in this paper for helping children become accustomed to hearing and using alternative ways of expressing themselves is one that is philosophically joined to those expressed by Bill Martin in his language series, *Sounds of Language Readers* (Holt, Rinehart and Winston), and by Sybil Marshall in *An Experiment in Education* (1966). Marshall says of her teaching methods:

I applied the theory which I followed generally in the teaching of English. It was based on the simple formula that if you stand out in the rain long enough, you are bound to get wet, and may even get soaked to the skin. I exposed my children to showers of English used for its true purpose. I never corrected grammar if by doing so I should have interrupted thought, for I consider that to be by far the more important . . . and always made a point of commenting favorably when anyone used a dialect phrase which was self-explanatory and vivid (134-35).

Divergent speech expressions

Osborn in his book, *Applied Imagination* (1960), quotes a senator who said, "We'll explore and deplore, only that and nothing more." To prevent that all-too-common predicament from being duplicated in this presentation, the rest of this paper concentrates on presenting some specific trade book resources as well as professional resources that may be used with children to help them adopt, when appropriate, some standard speech expressions that may be causing them difficulties. Because of space limitations, it is possible only to suggest a few library materials that their teachers can use creatively with their pupils to help them with their individual difficulties.

Because it is true that children are apt to read and write what they say, it seems logical to suppose that if we want to help them understand, speak, read, and write with ease the language of the mainstream culture, we should start with the language of the child.

First, a child must hear the words and language patterns we would like him to know and use (when they are appropriate) as alternatives for parts of his language. Second, he must be reinforced for using this convergent language (as well as reinforced for using the positive, divergent elements of his own dialect). He must not be punished for saying what is ordinarily normal and "correct" for him to say. As everyone knows "correct" is a very relative, subjective, and flexible term. As everyone knows, too, "punishment" can come in many guises.

If a child of a middle-class mother says, "I *seed Daddy* car, Mommy," Mommy does not punish the child or tell him he is wrong. She simply repeats in a most casual way the convergent expressions. She may say, for example, "Yes, that's right, you *saw* Dad*dy's* car." Teachers should use the same technique with their pupils.

The mother then usually gives the child many chances to hear, imitate, and use the convergent expressions. She does not expect perfection overnight. She rewards the child for his approximations of success. It is natural in terms of normal progress for any child who is in the process of learning any language to be able to understand words and patterns before he produces them. His first attempts at production normally will not be perfect productions but will be approximations of the model. A child must be given many opportunities to express himself orally, using those elements of the language that he may not feel "at home" in.

After presenting short stories and poems to children as a basic means of getting them joyfully attuned to some standard expressions that may be troublesome to them, teachers can initiate appropriate activities for their pupils. They should strive to avoid stereotyped fill-in-the-blank and cross-out-the-"wrong"-word ("wrong" to whom?) activities which are done individually in isolation. (Actually, assignments such as these should be described as "passivities," not activities.) In the examples of busywork which have just been mentioned, usually as much time is spent on the divergent stimuli as on the convergent stimuli.

In working with youngsters to enrich their language facilities, teachers should try to keep the children highly involved—and involved in oral-aural ways. In cumulative tales where there is great repetition of a standard expression, children should be encouraged to chime in. As much as possible, oral-aural games should be devised by the teacher and her pupils to reinforce what is being presented.

Many of the books listed in this paper are the kind that can stimulate children quite easily to start talking just by using the model standard expressions offered in the materials themselves. The materials suggested are ones both the children and the teacher can easily adapt, fly off from, and start creating from. They are meant to be oral language starters.

Working with *is* and *are*

Since some black children delete the words *is* and *are* from their speech, a teacher might want to plan some oral language activities to help these children use the words. To give children practice first in hearing these words, the teacher might read to them the book, *Some Things Are Scary,* by Heide and Van Clief. After reading the story, the teacher could tell the children some scary things—"Being alone at night *is* scary"; "Hearing the wind wail through the trees on a stormy night *is* scary." By giving a few examples, the teacher can help the children to open up and talk about what is scary to them. Their *volunteered* thoughts can be recorded on the board with their names attached to their contributions. Perhaps books containing the children's and the teacher's ideas can be duplicated for the whole group to read and keep. When children do open up and start telling their teacher what is scary to them, he can repeat, "Yes, that's scary," emphasizing the apostrophe -*s* structure which some black children have not been accustomed to hearing and, therefore, not accustomed to saying or reading. Naturally, it would be fun and helpful if the teacher would substitute other synonyms for *scary* and, occasionally, do it in a scary or dramatic way if he thinks the children would enjoy this sort of activity.

Naming a series of things that scare the children and the teacher is a perfect way for the children to repeat over and over again the word *are.* If children become accustomed to hearing *are* and saying *are,* they will be more apt to read it when they see the word in print.

It should be mentioned that when children (or adults, for that matter) are in the process of learning something new, they usually need more than a "hit-and-run" type of teaching. They do need repetition, but the repetition need not be unimaginative, deadly, or dull; instead it can be a delight both for the teacher and the children.

Teachers can and should structure their lessons to help children discover inductively what it is they want their pupils to learn. Reference lines of many kinds can be devised to help children see what their teachers want them to notice.

For example, when trying to get children to discover when to use *is* and when to use *are,* a teacher can read students the book by Krauss, *A Hole Is to Dig.* Later, he can ask the children for sentences they liked from the book. He can record them on the blackboard, putting all the *is* sentences on one side and the *are* sentences on the other side. He can underline all the nouns and draw a line or lines above them. Whether he draws one line above the nouns or more than one will depend on whether or not the nouns are singular or plural. He can then underline the *-s* in *is* and ask what the children-detectives have noted about the sentences.

A clue he can give is that *s* stands for *single,* and if a noun represents only one person or thing, it is single and must have an *-s* in the verb that goes with it—*is*. Later, children can make up their own sentences, orally using *is* and *are*. Again, a teacher might start by giving some examples and writing them on the blackboard as he says them: "*Dragons are* needed so that knights will always have jobs"; "The *sún* is so that each person can have his very own toaster." The teacher in his written examples might want to make the *s* in *is* huge so that it will really stand out. He might also suggest that his pupils do this in their written samples too, if they wish.

The same inductive technique and approach used in helping children with *is* and *are* can be used in helping children with *was* and *were, has* and *have,* and *does* and *do,* as well as in helping children to use the *-s* inflection on standard verbs in the present tense which are paired with third person singular subjects. An illustration of this pattern would be, "A *bóy* runs." Incidentally, children can be made aware that the indefinite articles *a* and *an* indicate that the following noun will be a singular one, and, if the verb is in the present tense, it will need an *-s*. When working with pronouns and the verb forms *is* and *are, was* and *were, has* and *have,* and *does* and *do,* teachers will need to make some minor adaptations which can be done quite easily. It goes without saying (almost) that children should be helped to succeed and rewarded when they do succeed.

It was interesting to read in *The New York Times Magazine* (April 4, 1971), an article entitled, "The Joy of Learning—In the Open Corridor," by Walter Schneir and Miriam Schneir. One idea emphasized was that it is possible to use ". . . the same material with children in different stages of learning development." This conviction is shared by the writer of this paper as well as by Eugene H. Smith (1969).

Hailstones and Halibut Bones by Mary O'Neill (1961), was used by an undergraduate student with young children in an inner-city school. One of the oral responses liked best came from a little boy who said, "The sound of red is 'YAHOO!'" Another student used the same book in an intermediate inner-city grade where the children never had poetry because "the teacher didn't have time for that." Here are two of the children's responses:

Green is grass in the summer time.
Green is color that does not easily rym.
Green is cool.
Green is quiet as a summer breeze.
Green is a color if you sneeze.
Green may be as lonely as it seems,
But if you like to daydream,
You would think of lime ice cream.

—Karen

Green is a leaf you just picked off of a tree,
Green is grass after a sweet April shower!
Green is a car that has a Grabber green color.
Green is a stem of a leaf that has broken off,
Green makes a trickling sound that whispers in
Green is a shirt that got in the dirt.

—Roxanne M.

When the student teacher returned to the class for her second teaching lesson with the same class of children, she had stenciled copies of all of their poems for them. They were thrilled. All of the children read each other's poems over and over again. The language they had used was elaborated language, and it all was salted and peppered heavily and correctly with *is*!

Here is a list of some resources to use with children to reinforce their hearing and saying the words *is* and *are*:

1. *Schools for Young Disadvantaged Children* by Ruth Hamlin, Rose Mukerji, and Margaret Yonemura. (New York: Columbia University, Teachers College Press, 1969), 47-51.

2. *That's What Friends Are For* by Florence Parry Heide and Sylvia Worth Van Clief, pictures by Brinton Turkle. (New York: Four Winds Press, 1968.)

3. *Some Things Are Scary* by Florence Parry Heide, pictures by Robert Osborn. (New York: Scholastic Book Services, 1969.)

4. *A Hole Is to Dig* by Ruth Krauss, pictures by Maurice Sendak. (New York: Harper and Brothers, 1952.)

5. *Frog, Where Are You?* by Mercer Mayer. (New York: Dial Press, 1969.)

6. *Hailstones and Halibut Bones* by Mary O'Neill. (New York: Doubleday, 1961.)

7. *Happiness Is a Warm Puppy* by Charles Schulz. (San Francisco: Determined Productions, 1962.)

8. *Snail, Where Are You?* by Tomi Ungerer. (New York: Harper and Brothers, 1962.)

9. "This Is the Way We Wash Our Hands," in *What Shall We Do and Allee Galloo* by Marie Winn, musical arrangements by Allan Miller, pictures by Karla Kuskin. (New York: Harper and Row, 1970.)

10. *Developing Language Programs for Young Disadvantaged Children* by Margaret Yonemura. (New York: Columbia University, Teachers College Press, 1969), 47-51.

The inflectional endings *-s* and *ed*

Some black children are not accustomed to using the *-s* inflection on present tense standard verbs when the verbs are accompanied by a third person singular subject. Previously, mention has been made of one approach that might be used to encourage children to put an *-s* marker on such verbs. Literary references that may strengthen each child's tendency to use this inflection include Evelyn Beyer's poem, "Jump or Jiggle," which can be found in "Time for Poetry" in the *Arbuthnot Anthology of Children's Literature* (Scott, Foresman, Chicago, 1961) and Donald J. Bissett's *Poems and Verses to Begin On* (Book 1, Chandler Publishing Company, San Francisco, 1967). Beyer's poem is composed of couplets such as "Frogs jump/ Caterpillars hump/ Worms wiggle/ Bugs jiggle. . . ." After reading, discussing, and possibly acting out this poem, the teacher could adapt Beyer's work by making the animals mentioned in the poem singular rather than plural. That is, the adapted lines would say, "A frog *jumps*/ A caterpillar _____."

It would be ideal for each child to have a copy of the poem as it appears in its adapted form. Then each child could write the new verb form as well as say it. Later, children could be helped by working with their teacher to create their own "Jump or Jiggle" poem. A teacher might start the children by putting on the board sample beginnings such as:

> A cow _____.
> A dog _____.
> A boy _____.
> A girl _____.

The children's own ideas could be dittoed for all to read and enjoy.

Another source to use when working with the third person singular -*s* inflection on standard verbs is the book, *What Do They Do When It Rains?* by Norman Bridwell (Scholastic Book Services, 1969). This very simple book can be used to get children to respond orally with the third person singular inflection of -*s* to the various questions posed. The book portrays different people engaged in the work they do when the sun is shining. A painter is shown painting the outside of a house, for example. Then the question is repeated again and again, "But what does he do when it rains?" Volunteers, beginning with the teacher who will provide the convergent model, can tell what they think various people do when it rains. The teacher should try to make it clear that many answers are possible and desirable. Thus, no child will feel that there is one right answer. This, in itself, should encourage children to let their thoughts pour out.

Other resources that teachers may want to use in helping children become aware of the third person singular -s inflection include the following materials:

1. "The Goblin" by Rose F. Fyleman in "Time for Poetry," *The Arbuthnot Anthology of Children's Literature.* (Chicago: Scott, Foresman, 1961), 142.

2. *Learning Action Words.* (Buffalo: Kenworthy Educational Service, 1954). This workbook with its pictures can be used to elicit inflectional endings some black children may not be accustomed to using. It can also be used to stimulate children to elaborate their language.

3. "Scholastic News Pilot Chart: Words About Moving," available from Scholastic Book Services, 50 West 44 Street, New York. This chart can be used not only to elicit the third person singular -s inflection from pupils but to elicit other inflectional endings such as -ed, and -ing as well.

4. "Help Yourself Picture Verbs, Frame Tray Puzzle," No. 4543. (Racine, Wisconsin: Whitman, 1969.) This inexpensive tool can be used in the same way as the materials published by Kenworthy Educational Service and Scholastic Book Services.

5. "I Speak, I Say, I Talk" by Arnold L. Shapiro, printed in *Childcraft* Library by Field Enterprises Educational Corporation, 510 Merchandise Mart Place, Chicago, Illinois 60654. This is a poem similar to Evelyn Beye's poem, "Jump or Jiggle," that can be easily adapted by the teacher to reinforce the third person singular inflection. It is also excellent to use to let children hear and say the -s marker on plural nouns.

Another inflection some black children may not use but which can hinder them in their language and reading comprehension is the -ed past tense ending on verbs. Children should be helped to realize that some words and phrases in our language indicate that some action has been completed, stopped, or finished. Expressions such as *yesterday, last year, previously,* and *a long time ago* should be brought to their attention. They can be told that words and phrases such as these often give clues that something has already happen*ed*.

One literary selection that can be used to get children to hear and say the *ed* ending with its various pronunciations is *I Know an Old Lady* by Rose Bonne, music by Alan Mills, pictures by Abner Graboff (Scholastic Book Services, 1961). This is a cumulative tale that has a generous supply of past tense -*ed* verbs in it. Since it is a cumulative tale, it won't be long before children are striving to remember the lines that are repeated over and over. They soon will find that they are joining in and saying the -*ed* endings that abound in this story.

A teacher should always be searching for poems, songs, or stories that repeat as regularly as waves roll in and out a standard expression which the children may not ordinarily be accustomed to hearing or saying. Then, after saying the lines together (voluntarily and joyfully), the teacher can provide the children with words they already know. The children with the teacher's help can make up new rhyming words to pair with the familiar words. That is, after working with *I Know an Old Lady* and using the pattern provided in this tale, the teacher might use the word *table* and say, "I know an old lady who swallowed a table. I don't know why she swallowed a table. I guess she's not stable." Or he might provide the word *cow* and ask the children to think with him of some lines for the story of the lady, using the word *cow* and rhyming words they might know. This technique is just one of many techniques that a teacher can use as a tool to help him give his children creative practice with language patterns.

Other trade book materials a teacher might want to read to his pupils to reinforce their understanding of the past tense marker -*ed* include the following:

1. *Why the Sun Was Late* by Benjamin Elkin, illustrated by Jerome Snyder. (New York: Parent's Magazine Press, 1966.) This is another cumulative tale which abounds in -*ed* endings and seems, by its very nature, to be the kind of book that makes the child want to join in and come too.

2. "How the Whale Got His Throat" from Rudyard Kipling's *Just So Stories.* This story can be read to children, and then their attention can be drawn to the delightful actions the Mariner busied himself with as soon as he found himself in the "whale's warm, dark, inside cupboards. . . ." The children can adapt the Mariner's actions using their own *-ed* words. They should be able to do this with the aid of their teacher after they discuss in a small group what they would do if they ever found themselves in a similar circumstance.

3. Jump-rope rhymes such as "Anthy Martha jump*ed* in the fire. . . ." from *Jump-Rope* Rhymes by Barbara McGee. (New York: Viking, 1968.)

References

Baratz, Joan C., and Shuy, Roger W. *Teaching Black Children to Read.* (Washington, D.C.: Center for Applied Linguistics, 1969.)

Cavin, Tony. *The Bright Red Porcupine.* (New York: Harlin Quist, 1969.)

Fasold, Ralph W., and Shuy, Roger W., Eds. *Teaching Standard English in the Inner City.* (Washington, D.C.: Center for Applied Linguistics, 1970.)

Goodman, Kenneth S. "Dialect Barriers to Reading Comprehension," *Teaching Black Children to Read,* Joan Baratz and Roger Shuy, Eds., 14-28. (Washington, D.C.: Center for Applied Linguistics, 1969.)

Johnson, Kenneth R. "Blacks," *Reading for the Disadvantaged: Problems of Linguistically Different Learners,* Thomas D. Horn, Ed., 29-38. (New York: Harcourt Brace Jovanovich, 1970.)

Labov, William. *The Study of Nonstandard English.* (Champaign, Illinois: National Council of Teachers of English, 1970.)

Larrick, Nancy, Ed. *On City Streets.* (New York: Bantam Books, 1969.)

Malcolm, Andrew H. "Reading Assists Youths' Speech," *New York Times,* May 9, 1971, 51.

Marshall Sybil. *An Experiment in Education.* (New York: Cambridge University Press, 1966.)

O'Neill, Mary. *Hailstones and Halibut Bones.* (New York: Doubleday, 1961.)

Osborn, Alex F. *Applied Imagination: Principles and Procedures of Creative Problem-Solving.* (New York: Charles Scribner's Sons, 1960.)

Riessman, Frank. *Helping the Disadvantaged Pupil to Learn More Easily.* (Englewood Cliffs, New Jersey: Prentice-Hall, 1966.)

Schneir, Walter, and Schneir, Miriam. "The Joy of Learning—in the Open Corridor," *New York Times Magazine,* April 4, 1971, 30-31, 72-80, 92-93, 96-98.

Smith, E. Brooks; Goodman, Kenneth S.; and Meredith, Robert. *Language and Thinking in the Elementary School.* (New York: Holt, Rinehart and Winston, 1970.)

Smith, Eugene H. *Teacher Preparation in Composition.* (Champaign, Illinois: National Council of Teachers of English, 1969.)

Torrance, E. Paul. "Creative Positives of Disadvantaged Children and Youth," *The Gifted Child Quarterly,* 13 (Summer 1969), 71-81.

PUBLISHING NONSTANDARD DIALECT MATERIALS

NEUTRALIZING THE EFFECT
OF THE NONSTANDARD DIALECT

Dorothy Z. Seymour
Ginn and Company
Boston, Massachusetts

Educators and publishers are continually discovering more ways in which black disadvantaged children have been victims of unintended discrimination in the schools. Perhaps the most striking example of discrimination is the spotty treatment of important blacks in history texts. But discrimination also exists in reading. In books that teach reading, one problem recognized in the fifties was lack of inclusion of blacks or unrealistic treatment of them in stories. Finally, in the late sixties, educators and publishers discovered that many black children suffer discrimination in reading class because of their language.

It seems pretty well substantiated by now that gross differences between a child's oral language and the language he finds symbolized in instructional material can retard progress in learning to read (Baratz and Baratz, 1969; Labov, 1967). In the past few years, several linguists have been able to describe for us many of the crucial phonological and morphological differences between so-called black English and standard English. Some of these are so striking as to include different sentence order or different vocabulary or differences in the presence or absence of a particular word. Other differences are in use of sounds, sound clusters, and tense person markers (Fasold and Wolfram, 1970; NCTE, 1968).

Different solutions

Experimenters have proposed different solutions for dealing with this mismatch between oral language and print. The preparation of so-called dialect readers is one solution. This stratagem provides the reader with printed words that are much more likely to match his speech (Baratz, 1969). One of the big problems in adopting such readers is that many black parents disapprove of it. They seem to prefer that their children not see reinforced in print a dialect which has no standing with the American middle class (Labov, 1968; Seymour, 1971). Proof that seeing deviant speech represented in print has shock value is the fact that this sentence printed in inch-high letters was used as an attention-getter in a recent *New York Times* ad (1968):

> De chirren trawl to de scream ta see
> de frinly snail.

The deviant spellings shown here were used to draw attention to the ad in the same way sex or vulgarities are used.

A psychological and sociological fact such as the commonly low opinions of the dialect has to be taken into account in the preparation of instructional materials. Scholars and teachers may deplore the fact that seeing the dialect in print is a shock, but they cannot ask parents or publishers to ignore that fact. More important, there is a serious question as to whether dialect readers are necessary in order to teach black ghetto youngsters to read (Goodman, 1969; Venezky, 1970). There are other approaches.

Avoidance technique

One approach that should be considered was used by the publishers of a new basal series. Bear in mind that the new program was not prepared for ghetto youngsters. It is a general series, directed to the general market. The teacher is to use it at a slow, medium, or fast pace, depending on how quickly her students can accomplish the objectives of the program. Since disadvantaged black youngsters are among those who would be using the program, the authors and editors took their language into account in preparing the series and made special provision for them where it seemed possible to do so. The approach taken was based on what some authorities call an "avoidance technique"

(Shuy, 1969; Wolfram, 1970). To carry it out, each lesson in the word analysis program was tested against rules based on certain phonemic and morphemic differences between Negro nonstandard speech and the standard dialect, ones that seemed important and that could be dealt with in a general series.

To explain how these rules were applied, it is first necessary to consider how word analysis is taught and the way this instruction can penalize the speaker of a nonstandard dialect.

Auditory perception

Instructional techniques in word analysis often begin with auditory perception of language sounds. In order to establish a phoneme-grapheme correspondence—e.g., a vowel correspondence —a teacher must be sure that the learner understands which language sound is under consideration. Thus, the teacher reads aloud many word examples containing the sound. For example, when he is trying to establish the connection between the vowel sound in *miss* with the letter *i*, he may ask the students to listen for the vowel sounds in the words *Bill, mitt, risk, tip, pick, big, list*, etc. The learner should also be able to hear the difference between the vowel sound under consideration and a different one, so words with other vowel sounds are given as foils, and the learner develops and demonstrates his auditory skill by selecting only those words containing the vowel sound under consideration. The pupils may be asked to choose the word with the vowel sound of *miss* from among words like *pin, men*, and *pen*.

In such a case the ghetto youngster is going to be penalized, because in his dialect there is probably no contrast between the sounds /i/ and /e/ before nasals like /n/ (Fasold and Wolfram, 1970; NCTE, 1968): *pin* and *men* may rhyme in his dialect, and *pin* and *pen* may be homophones. However, if the list is changed to delete the nasal consonant sounds and to offer words with strongly contrasting vowel sounds, he should have no difficulty in making the necessary discrimination.

In the new reading program, the child who has no contrast between *pin* and *pen* is not asked to hear what for him is a nonexistent difference. Instead, in word lists for auditory perception of the vowel sounds /i/ or /e/ the sounds are contrasted with other sounds, as illustrated in this word list from an early first grade teachers' manual (Clymer and Parr, 1969):

sit, sat, sick, pill, pat, pick
will, with, walk, tick, tock, tip.

You will note that the learner is asked to pick out words with the vowel sound /i/ from among others with /æ/, /a/, and /ɔ/, not /e/, and there are no nasals following the vowel sounds in these words.

The strategy used here assists speakers of other dialects too. There are geographical groups other than speakers of Negro nonstandard English who have no contrast between these vowel sounds.

This avoidance strategy need not be carried out in every subsequent lesson on the correspondence. It is only in the earliest lessons on a particular sound that avoidance seems really essential. After the correspondence has been established, avoidance is less important because the child has already made the connection between sound and letter and has used this information in analyzing printed words; by that time slight ambiguities are less likely to be confusing.

Consonants and consonant clusters

Another instance in which an avoidance strategy is effective is in establishing sound-symbol correspondences for certain initial consonants. Here again, auditory perception is the first step. In the new program when the sound heard at the beginning of *then* was introduced in order to establish its correspondence with the letters *th*, the word lists for auditory perception were carefully checked so the foils did not contain the consonant sound at the beginning of *doll*, since in the Negro nonstandard dialect that sound is often used where speakers of the standard use the voiced "th" sound /ð/. In addition, word lists used for perception and discrimination of this sound in medial word-position were checked to see that they did not contain the medial consonant sound in *ever*, since speakers of Negro nonstandard often use this sound medially where speakers of the standard use the voiced "th" /ð/ (Fasold and Wolfram, 1970; NCTE, 1968).

Instruction in final consonant clusters also requires special attention when using the avoidance strategy. Consonant clusters are introduced after the pupils have already learned to read words with single consonants. Therefore, the lessons generally include some independent work in which the children demonstrate their mastery of decoding words with the cluster.

From the point of view of standard English, black English "reduces" a number of final clusters; for example /ft/ is reduced to /f/—that is, *stuffed* sounds like *stuff*; /nd/ is reduced to /n/—*grand* sounds like *gran*; /ks/ is reduced to /k/—*tax* sounds like *tack*; and /st/ is reduced to /s/—*lost* sounds like *loss* (Fasold and Wolfram, 1970; NCTE, 1968). Therefore, if the learner is given as a foil a word which is phonologically a cluster reduction, he might easily choose the answer with the reduction, particularly if it occurs first in the list. For example:

On Sunday Mr. Older was

our _____ for dinner.

guess guest

If the child decodes the word *guess* first, as he is likely to do, he is likely to think it represents the word that means a person to whom hospitality is extended, and he may look no further. Therefore, in this kind of exercise he is being penalized not for being unable to read but simply for speaking a different dialect.

The way this penalty can be avoided is to offer only words with clusters as possible answers, as in these sentences from an exercise in the teachers' manual for the Level 8 book in the new program (Clymer and Ruddell, 1969):

To provide practice in decoding and using words whose final sounds are /lt/, /ft/, and /pt/, distribute this worksheet.

Directions: Add the letters *ft, lt,* or *pt* to finish the words in these sentences.

lt	ft	pt

1. The children le *ft* the party at ten o'clock.
2. The man swe · *pt* the shop floor every night.
3. The sun made the ice cream me *lt* .
4. Dad put on the new be *lt* we gave him.
5. Each person put a gi *ft* on the table.
6. The little girl we *pt* when she lost her puppy.
7. The baby cre *pt* under the chair.
8. Mother put sa *lt* on the meat.
9. The man fe *lt* better soon.
10. The rocket was ready for li *ft* -off.

Note that final clusters are contrasted not with single final consonants but with other clusters. Here are some sentences from a similar exercise on clusters, this time from the new basal reading workbook, Level 6 (Clymer and Jones, 1969):

1. _____ up!   Mend
                          Stand

2. His dad plays in the _____. ˙   band
                                              mend

3. Do jets _____ at the airport?   band
                                               land

4. The boys will stay in a _____.   bent
                                                tent

5. He _____ his pal a postcard.   sent
                                              bent

Note that words with final *nd* are contrasted not with final *n* but with words with the same cluster or other clusters the child can decode.

Tense and person markers

The avoidance technique is also useful when giving instruction in the reading of words with tense and person markers. For purposes of reading, children must be taught that in English writing the letters *ed* form the regular marker for the past tense of most verbs. The way this was traditionally demonstrated to children can be seen in these sentences from a 1966 exercise, in which pupils had to show their understanding by completing the sentences with the verbs that finish them correctly—"correctly" meaning "by using standard grammar" (Ousley and Russell).

                chatter
1. The monkey   chattered   all the time.
                chattering

          open
2. Jean   opened   the door.
          opening

             crawl
3. The turtle   crawled   to the pond.
             crawling

And here is a selection from a 1965 exercise of the same type (Richardson, Smith, and Weiss):

1. Spunky's nap _____ with Vicky's yelling.
              end   ending   ended

2. The ham was _____ to Spunky.
            toss   tosses   tossed

3. Mrs. Everly _____ to step into the kitchen.
          pretending   pretended

Note that in these sentences the pupil who speaks Negro nonstandard might choose the first answer because it would "sound right" to him, since in his dialect the sounds we represent with the *-ed* ending often are not used.

In contrast, look at these sentences from an exercise in the new program's Level 5 teacher's manual (Clymer and Wyatt, 1969).

Add *d* to each word and read it. Then write one of the words in the blanks:

shave   name   stare

1. The boys _____ the pet grasshopper Mr. Jump.
2. All the people _____ at the white elephant.
3. Dad got up and found something to eat. Then he _____.

In this exercise all the answers are already inflected. This kind of exercise, besides avoiding a penalty on the speaker of Negro nonstandard, has two additional advantages: 1) it requires the child to read the entire word, not merely to look for the one with (or without) *-ed*, and 2) it gives extra experience in observing words with *-ed* and the past tense.

Plurals and possessives

This same kind of language difference should be taken into account when giving reading instruction in plurals with *-s*, in second-person verb forms with *-s*, and possessives with *'s*, where speakers of Negro nonstandard do not use the sound represented in the dialect by the letter *s*.

Look at some examples from this 1966 exercise which purports to reinforce the reading of words that indicate plurals. Actually, what it does is require the pupil to respond on the basis of his oral grammar (Ousley and Russell).

Write the following material on the chalkboard. Have the children decide which form of the word belongs in each sentence. Ask one child to draw a line around the correct word form and another child to read the sentence aloud using the correct word.

                                     cake

Mother will make a _____.   cakes

                         chair

We like to paint _____.   chairs

                  hat

We have funny _____.   hats

                  tree

Tiger ran up the _____.   trees

                  kitten

Tiger is a good _____.   kittens

To the speaker of Negro nonstandard, the sentences "We like to paint chair" and "We have funny hat" might sound perfectly all right, so he could be trapped into getting those sentences wrong. Another exercise, one published in 1965, includes these sentences (Black, et al.):

1. Two _____ are in the street.
      boy   boys
2. All the street _____ go on.
      light   lights
3. Ann had many _____.
      book   books
4. Carmen had two _____.
      cat   cats

The pupil who can read the base form of the words but may not use the sound represented by the s in these words is not likely to do well on this exercise.

The same problem can be seen in this 1966 exercise on verb forms with and without the letter s. You can see that the pupil who speaks Negro nonstandard, even if he can read the words, might be discriminated against because of his grammar (Ousley and Russell).

Structural Analysis. To develop the child's ability to distinguish the verb and its s form, distribute duplicated copies of the exercise shown here.

Tom _____ the pets.   like
The pets _____ Tom.   likes

Tom _____ Pony.   ride
See Tom _____.   rides

We _____ Tiger.   want
Tiger _____ Cathy.   wants

Tom and Betty can _____.   paint
Susan _____ a chair.   paints

Again some children are likely to write "Tom like the pets" and "Tom ride Pony," not because they cannot read but because their grammar does not specify -s inflections in these cases. In contrast, look at this exercise from the new program (Clymer and Wyatt, 1969):

quacks   sleeps   backs

1. That duck ＿＿＿＿＿＿ all the time.
2. Dad ＿＿＿＿＿＿ the car out to the street.
3. Pete ＿＿＿＿＿＿ in that bed.

And note this exercise, which offers reinforcement of decoding inflected and uninflected words but compares only like forms (Clymer and Wyatt, 1969):

1. James is ＿＿＿＿＿＿＿＿＿ his mother at home.
   working   helping
2. Ken said, "I can't play. I have ＿＿＿＿＿＿ to do."
                                    work   help
3. Mop ＿＿＿＿＿＿ the boys.
       helps   works
4. James ＿＿＿＿＿＿ his father.
   worked   helped

Summary

In summary, then, it is possible to make special provision in a general reading series for language differences between speakers of black English and of the standard dialect. The differences that can be handled are both phonological and morphological. Avoidance strategies for phonological differences are:

1. Don't require the learner to hear a contrast between the vowel sounds of *pin* and *pen*. Instead, use word examples with vowel sounds that contrast, particularly before nasals.
2. Don't offer words with initial /d/ as in *den* as foils when giving instruction in the letter correspondence for initial

/ð/ as in *then*, or words with medial /v/ as in *never* when giving instruction in medial /ð/ as in *neither*. Instead, offer word examples that contain other consonant sounds in these positions.

3. In teaching the decoding of certain final consonant clusters, don't offer words with cluster reductions as foils; e.g., for /nd/ as in *and* don't use /n/ as in *an;* for /ks/ as in *tax* don't use /k/ as in *tack;* and for /st/ as in *lost* don't use /s/ as in *loss.* Instead, give word examples that use the full cluster or other clusters.

Comparable avoidance strategies for morphological differences are:

1. When presenting exercises that give practice in decoding verbs inflected with *-ed*, make all the choice words with (or without) the inflections; e.g., offer a choice between *work* and *walk* or *worked* and *walked*, not between *work* and *worked* or *walk* and *walked*.

2. In presenting exercises for practice in decoding third person singular verbs inflected with *-s*, offer a choice between inflected verbs like *helps* and *hops* or uninflected verbs like *help* and *hop*.

3. Use the same technique in dealing with plurals inflected with *-s*: offer a choice between different nouns, both inflected as in *chairs* and *chains*, or both uninflected as in *chair* and *chain*.

4. Finally, use the same strategy when presenting an exercise in decoding possessives: make the choice one between two nouns with *'s* or two without.

The avoidance strategy also seems to have implications for the field of testing. When the teacher administers a reading test, he wants to know how complete the child's mastery of reading is. If many of the items on the test are going to test the child's grammatical style rather than his reading ability, the test results are simply not as valid as they could be and not as helpful to the teacher for placement, grouping, or instructional planning. Tests used for such important purposes should be carefully scrutinized to see that they are really testing reading mastery and not mastery of standard grammar.

The points being made by the use of the avoidance strategy are these:

1. Exercises in auditory perception which test nonexistent differences in sound should be adjusted to include word examples of sounds which contrast in most Americans' speech.

2. Exercises which purport to give reading instruction but which actually test a child's use of standard grammar should be changed so that a child who can read but whose natural grammar is not standard will not be penalized inadvertently.

3. Reading is not necessarily the best place to teach the use of the standard dialect. The decision as to whether standard speech is to be taught or expected should and can be made separately from a decision on what kind of reading instruction is to be given.

References

Baratz, Joan C. "Teaching Reading in an Urban Negro School System," *Teaching Black Children to Read,* Joan Baratz and Roger Shuy, Eds., 92-116. (Washington, D.C.: Center for Applied Linguistics, 1969.)

Baratz, Stephen S., and Baratz, Joan C. "Negro Children and Urban Education: A Cultural Solution," *Social Education,* 33 (April 1969), 401-04.

Black, Ira Simonton, et al., Ed. Teachers' Annotated Edition of *More About Around the City,* Bank Street Readers. (New York: Macmillan, 1965), 78.

Clymer, Theodore, and Jones, Virginia W. Teachers' edition, Skills Handbook *Seven Is Magic,* Reading 360. (Boston: Ginn, 1969), 31.

Clymer, Theodore, and Parr, Billie. Teachers' edition, *A Duck Is a Duck*, Reading 360. (Boston: Ginn, 1969), 83.

Clymer, Theodore, and Ruddell, Robert B. Teachers' edition, *How It Is Nowadays*, Reading 360. (Boston: Ginn, 1969), 247.

Clymer, Theodore, and Wyatt, Nita M. Teachers' edition, *May I Come In?* Reading 360. (Boston: Ginn, 1969), 111, 218-19, 241-42.

Fasold, Ralph W., and Wolfram, Walt. "Some Linguistic Features of Negro Dialect," *Teaching Standard English in the Inner City*, Ralph Fasold and Roger Shuy, Eds., 41-86. (Washington, D.C.: Center for Applied Linguistics, 1970.)

Goodman, Kenneth. "Dialect Barriers," *Teaching Black Children to Read*, Joan Baratz and Roger Shuy, Eds., 14-28. (Washington, D.C.: Center for Applied Linguistics, 1969).

Labov, William. "The Non-Standard Vernacular of the Negro Community: Some Practical Suggestions," *Position Papers from Language Education for the Disadvantaged*, Report 3. (Washington, D.C.: N.D.E.A., June 1968.)

Labov, William. "Some Sources of Reading Problems for Negro Speakers of Nonstandard English," reprint from NCTE, *New Directions in Elementary English*. (Champaign, Illinois: NCTE, 1967.)

National Council of Teachers of English. *Nonstandard Dialect*. (New York: Board of Education, 1968.) *New York Times*, December 31, 1968.

Ousley, Odille, and Russell, David H. Manual for the Primer, to accompany *The Little White House*, 100 Edition. (Boston: Ginn, 1966), 140-171.

Ousley, Odille, and Russell, David H. Manual for the Second Reader—1, to accompany *We Are Neighbors*, 100 Edition. (Boston: Ginn, 1966), 141, 253, 307.

Richardson, Jack E., Jr.; Smith, Henry Lee, Jr.; and Weiss, Bernard J. *Letters, Patterns, and Drills* for *It Happens on a Ranch*. (New York: Harper and Row, 1965), 56.

Seymour, Dorothy Z. "Black Children, Black Speech," *Commonweal*, 95 (November 19, 1971), 175-78.

Shuy, Roger W. "Whatever Happened to the Way Kids Talk?" unpublished paper read before the National Conference on the Language Arts, April 1969.

Venezky, Richard L. "Nonstandard Language and Reading," *Elementary English*, 47 (March 1970), 334-45.

Wolfram, Walt. "Sociolinguistic Alternatives in Teaching Reading to Nonstandard Speakers," *Reading Research Quarterly*, 6 (Fall 1970), 9-33.

A NONSTANDARD PUBLISHER'S PROBLEMS

JUSTIN M. FISHBEIN
Science Research Associates
Chicago, Illinois

Juan is nine and lives in a dusty Arizona town. Isaiah is thirteen and lives in a roach-ridden Harlem flat; James is eleven and lives with his Tlingit Indian parents and relatives in a Juneau (Alaska) shack.

These children live miles from one another and have quite different lifestyles. Yet these children have four things in common. Each is an American; each is a member of a working-class family. Each speaks only in a nonstandard dialect of English. And each has a teacher who is begging a bookman for instructional materials to teach these children to understand, speak, read, and write standard English.

In Arizona, a teacher complains: "These Chicano children lack the experiential background necessary for classroom success." In Harlem, a portly black teacher observes that "most of these black youngsters are nonverbal. They don't know their sounds. No wonder they have trouble learning to read." In Juneau, a white teacher who has moved there from Oregon contends that because of the way these Indian children talk, "nobody will give them a decent job." Then she does what she considers to be a favor for them: she refuses to let them answer questions unless they use standard English.

Mulling over this situation, the textbook publisher concludes that opportunity is knocking. Heed the teachers' plea for materials to teach standard English. Uplift the kids; solve social problems; do well by doing good. There's a need; now fill it.

On the surface, it all seems so simple, too simple. For one thing, publishing is not what it used to be. There was a time when the word *house* properly described the publisher's place of business. Often it was a converted mansion. That meant incandescent bulbs in lamps, throw rugs on the floors, cluttered desks, pipe smoke, sherry and dark scotch, overstuffed leather chairs, the leisurely lunch. You get the picture. There were relatively few book buyers and even fewer bookstores.

This was the publisher of McGuffey's day. McGuffey wrote his graded readers himself. His publisher paid him a royalty of 10 percent until McGuffey's earnings reached a thousand dollars. At that point, the readers became the absolute property of the publisher. Over the next hundred years they were revised five times and sold more than 122 million copies. The publisher was able to select a property that called for virtually no development funds and no royalty; reproduce it at minimal expense, including revision costs; and circulate it to the widest possible market over a long period of time. In this way, he was able to keep the sales price way down and still make a profit.

Today, textbook publishing is different. Turning out a textbook series takes more than a McGuffey. It may require teams of people—scholars, classroom teachers, media specialists. Someone has to assemble these people as a group, give them a task orientation, keep them working together harmoniously. Someone has to make certain that a publishable product results from their efforts. Artists, illustrators, book designers—a host of specialists may be involved. Someone has to pay them for their time and talent, believing that the resulting product can be published profitably. That someone usually is a publisher. His product may require casebound books, paperbound books, spirit masters, boxes, sound filmstrips, cassettes, colored pencils, and many other components. In other words, it may require a substantial, high-risk investment. Publishers usually will spend a considerable amount of energy considering this risk before reaching a decision.

They'll take a close look at the market. It's not the same today as it was in McGuffey's time. In those days, one textbook series might have been all that was needed for a melting-pot society. The view was that the downtrodden and poor, the homeless of other nations, would blend together into a vibrant homogenized multitude. Assimilation was the watchword. Old World ethnic and cultural identity had to be subordinated quickly and without protest to the American way. Our normative order put pressure to conform on all immigrants, and culture conflict occurred when children began to feel embarrassed by parents who maintained the ways of the Old World, including its eating and linguistic habits. You didn't eat garlic, and you didn't talk the Old World tongue. Anyone who was ignorant of the American way was recognized at once as a "greenhorn." Whether through garlic or language, you betrayed yourself every time you opened your mouth. Therefore you spoke English, and where your social status was related to the numbers of generations in this nation, you sprinkled your speech with the latest expressions.

That was the environment that enabled a publisher to select a manuscript such as that of the McGuffey readers, reproduce it without the need for a substantial investment, and circulate it to the widest possible audience for a number of generations. Selection, reproduction, and circulation: that's what publishing is all about.

Today, with the population explosion and the call for universal literacy, you'd think that it would again be a McGuffey heyday. Well, it isn't. Possibly because the flow of in-migration was curtailed during the Twenties, we are no longer other-directed; that is, we're no longer nationalistic in our outlook. We are no longer a melting pot. Instead, we are inner-directed. We are not just a nation aware of its states; we are a society aware of its cultures. We are pluralistic. Our society used to seek the homogenization of various cultures and ethnic groups, but today we recognize the right to coexistence of culturally autonomous groups.

For the textbook publisher who requires a mass audience, a fragmented market of autonomous cultures is not nearly as attractive as the mass market of McGuffey's day.

And this market threatens to become even more fragmented. Suppose, for instance, that instructional materials have to be published for each of the three hundred major Indian tribes. What if there must be one set of materials for the Sioux and another for the Chippewa? The materials would cost as much to develop as a mass audience program would, but the return would be infinitesimal.

Or consider the need for instructional materials for Spanish speaking Americans. The number of Spanish speaking Americans is estimated at from 9-to-12½ million. But this total isn't what it seems. It has to be fragmented, subdivided into various age groups. For example, we would not expect the interests of an eight-year-old Spanish speaking child to be the same as those of a Spanish speaking adult. To make matters worse, there are other splinters to consider. Some Spanish speaking Americans are poor; their lifestyle isn't the same as that of more affluent Spanish speaking Americans. Some migrate annually; others do not. Some are from Puerto Rico, some from Cuba, some from the Bahamas, some from Mexico. The Puerto Rican's cultural heritage is different from the Mexican's, etc. In some places, Chicanos are in the majority; in other places they're not. How is a publisher to meet each individual need?

Then there's the situation with black English. In March 1971, for example, many teachers attending a Purdue University conference thought that they were to weigh the question, English: black and white? However, in an opening address, Orlando Taylor of the Center for Applied Linguistics asserted that "the real purpose of this conference is to discuss the language of black folks and its implications for education."

There was no implication; there was a strident call: accept black English; don't demand standard English. Barry D. Amis of Michigan State University told the audience that "black English is vibrant; standard English is opaque."

All this makes it even harder for a publisher to decide what to do. How do you transcribe black English in instances where it is phonologically different from standard English? Or maybe you don't. Is black English in Boston the same as that in New York? Is New York's the same as that of Chicago? Is Chicago's the same as that of Detroit? Is Detroit's the same as that of Phoenix, Arizona? Is black English the same for each black socioeconomic class? If one black English is different from the next, is there a standard black English? Which black English do you choose? And what about blacks who don't speak or understand "standard" black English? Should there be materials to teach them to understand and speak black English, so they won't be regarded as Uncle Toms?

The individualized needs in the market, lessening the opportunities for mass publishing, are only part of the problem facing the publisher. Another stems from the question being debated about the propriety of publishing anything at all. For example, it is argued that since tests use standard English, they do not validly evaluate the achievements of persons who do not perform in standard English. Taylor argued that teachers should stop using them and should do the hard-nosed work necessary to develop more valid instruments. Should publishers stop publishing these tests before new instruments are available?

Kenneth Goodman sounded a humanist note, arguing that schools should stop trying to turn out all Kens and Barbies. We educators ought to accept the language that children bring to school, regardless of its social status, he continued. He rejected the interventionist stand that the only way to succeed in society is to command standard English and condemned persons who advocate behavior modification for their "viscious attacks on children." He declared: "We must root the behavior changers out of the temples of learning." Now any publisher, aware that tax-supported agencies buy his materials and aware of the intense ethnic pride of vocal minorities, will think long and hard before deciding whether to publish materials to enable persons to acquire the ability to understand and speak standard English. Some school systems shy away from controversial materials of instruction. And this all assumes that someone can develop materials that will enable persons to change from nonstandard to standard English.

But there's more to this issue of ethnic pride. At the IRA Kansas City convention, Stewart and Baratz suggested that blacks should be taught to read with materials in black dialect. Recall the howls of indignation from some black educators at the insinuation that black youngsters need something special to be able to learn to read, something that whites don't need.

Or consider a young English teacher at Purdue. She noted that parents of her black students complained because they didn't have to buy as many paperback books as parents of white students did. What do black parents think about nonstandard English? Here's what one parent thinks:

SAVE OUR LANGUAGE

As a taxpayer, I favor teachers getting a salary increase and better teaching facilities. I am also for weeding out about 75 percent of the teachers—those who are poorly trained or not trained at all.

Last week, when visiting a public school, I heard a number of teachers speaking incorrectly. They said, "I axed" (for "I asked") and "I be" (for "I am"), and added an "s" to "men" and "women" and left it off "cents." How did such people pass their examinations? Who were their examiners? Did they pay their way in?

I am a Chicago-born Negro who attended Chicago public schools 60 years ago, when we had teachers (whatever their subject) who taught pupils to speak correctly. Let's again teach our children to speak correctly. Save our beautiful English language. Mrs. R. O.

(*The Chicago Tribune*, March 6, 1971)

There are three other factors to be considered. The first is parochialism. Some of the research on nonstandard English is being carried out by one research team in one part of the country and another research team in another part of the country. Are they working cooperatively, sharing information? Generally speaking, these research groups are proud of their accomplishments. However, one group is not likely to advocate usage of materials developed by another. Each seems to be parochial in its approach to research. So Expert A says that something is all right for the XYZ school system but not right for the ABC school system. Will New York public schools buy materials developed by the Chicago Public Schools and vice versa? It's something to think about, because parochialism may make investments in research and development less attractive.

The second is whether our argument about language and socioeconomic class is germane to more fundamental questions. The argument seems to go something like this. One side contends that members of minority groups face discrimination in part because of the language they use. Therefore equip them with standard English, and this will eliminate one cause of discrimination. The other side counters that nonstandard English is all right as is. Therefore what's really needed is to convince the dominant majority to accept nonstandard English.

Each side is lots of fun to weigh—very aesthetic—but is either one germane to finding solutions to the underlying causes of prejudices in society? Does the use of language represent patterns of thought? Does the use of words represent experience? What are the personality and intellectual, or cognitive, correlates of standard English usage? Perhaps research is needed to provide information about the questions being debated by Piaget, Bruner, and Chomsky on the relations between experience, innate cognitive structures, cognitive development, and language competence.

The third factor relates to social mobility. Studies of social class in America indicate that language is only one aspect of socioeconomic class. Others include religion, race, occupation, residence, and belonging to the "right" groups. Often, persons who are upwardly mobile start behaving like persons in socioeconomic classes in which they want to be accepted. For some, one such trait is language. Still, talking like Mrs. Gotrocks doesn't mean that she'll accept you as a peer. Is it conceivable that as America becomes increasingly stratified, upward mobility is more difficult? If it is, then does the dominant majority seriously consider arguments by the minority to "accept us as we are"? Probably not. At the Purdue conference Raven McDavid noted that Londoners did not accept the Northumbrians until the northerners became rich. Then the Londoners accepted not only the Northumbrians but also their language. Perhaps this suggests that nonstandard English is not as much of a factor in prejudice as we believe. It may suggest that adherence to other norms, values, traits, and attributes of society is more important. Is it racist to suggest that behavior conforming to the norms of the majority in a society will lead to acceptance? If a minority rejects the values of a society, it will unquestionably have its own normative order, and this order itself may encourage the formation and development of the minority's own patois, like the secret greetings of a lodge.

Publishers probably would agree that lodges need books, too, but because the volume is low, the prices are high.

For Juan, Isaiah, and James, as well as their teachers, standard and nonstandard dialects of English are genuine problems. Maybe nonstandard dialect really matters and maybe it doesn't, just like attitudes toward garlic forty years ago. Time, and perhaps research, will tell.

As for the publisher, because attitudes and concerns are divided and in transition—and because what little research there is, is so inconclusive—the publishing opportunities are not very attractive.

But publishing does have an important role to play right now. It can select topics such as this one and statements about these topics; it can reproduce them, and it can circulate them widely to educators and the general public. In this way it can generate discussion and perhaps the development of a consensus. Perhaps after developing awareness of this problem, publishing will spur development of a workable solution.

REVIEWING SOME ISSUES
AND PRINCIPLES

LANGUAGE AND COGNITION:

Current Perspectives From Linguistics and Psychology

JOHN B. CARROLL
Educational Testing Service
Princeton, New Jersey

In a series of papers published in the late 1950s and early 1960s, the British sociologist Basil Bernstein (1958, 1962) proposed a distinction between two forms of language that has caught the attention of educators and educational psychologists on both sides of the Atlantic. One form is what he called "public" language, the other is what he called "formal" language. Later, he renamed these forms as the "restricted" code and the "elaborated" code, respectively. It was not Bernstein's drawing of the distinction between these two forms of language that was of particular moment; it was what Bernstein said about them, namely that the "public" or "restricted" code tended to be limited to short, highly stereotyped utterances whose symbolism is descriptive and concrete; whereas, the "formal" or "elaborated" language is rich in qualification and complexity. The implication was that the user of the "restricted" code is unable to convey any careful, logical analysis of a situation or even to conceive of a situation in any analytic terms; whereas, the user of the "formal" or "elaborated" code is not so handicapped. In a number of empirical studies, Bernstein claimed to have been able to demonstrate the existence of these two types of language and to show their correlation with social-class differentiation.

Actually, Bernstein's views on the difference between these two codes and the effect of the difference on thinking have never been entirely clear and, as has been pointed out by Lawton (1968), these views have undergone certain changes in emphasis over the course of years. Lawton believes that Bernstein did not really mean to say that the linguistic code actually influences the form of thought; rather he argued that thought, and the kind of language used to express that thought, is a function of the social situation and the individual's perception of his role in society. Lawton also points out that the alleged correlation between language code and social class is not as great as some of those who quote Bernstein might have us think: on occasion, lower-class persons can use the "elaborated" code, and even in Bernstein's early presentations of his theory, it was emphasized that middle-class persons use both the "restricted" code and the "elaborated" code, depending upon the social situation.

Be that as it may, Bernstein's ideas have been much discussed. As frequently happens when new ideas are discussed by people who hear about them only second-hand, Bernstein's ideas have been watered down, modified, and oversimplified. It has been assumed that Bernstein's "restricted" code is one in which it is impossible to formulate thought of any high degree of logical complexity, and it has also been assumed that lower-class persons, being limited to the use of a "restricted" code, are unable to formulate logical thought. Bernstein did not make any such simplistic claims. I refer you to Lawton's analysis of Bernstein's writings for a more accurate statement of what Bernstein actually said.

In their book *Teaching Disadvantaged Children in the Pre-School*, Bereiter and Engelmann (1966) cited Bernstein's theories as claiming that "the speech of lower-class people follows a linguistic code . . . that is inadequate for expressing personal or original opinions, for analysis and careful reasoning, for dealing with anything hypothetical or beyond the present, and for explaining anything very complex." According to these writers, Bernstein "sees the [lower-class] child . . . as being trapped by the restrictions of [his] linguistic code and unable to operate at the high conceptual and logical level that is required in formal education." They go on to describe the "language problems of culturally deprived children" (i.e., lower-class black children), making such points as these:

1. "The speech of the severely deprived children seems to consist not of distinct words, but rather of whole phrases or sentences that function like giant words . . . . These 'giant word' units cannot be taken apart by the child and recombined . . . . Instead of saying 'He's a big dog,' the deprived child says 'He bih daw.' Instead of saying 'I ain't got no juice,' he says 'Uai-ga-na-ju!'"

2. It is not merely a problem of "faulty pronunciation," but of an "inability to deal with sentences *as sequences of meaningful parts*" (italics in the original). The lower-class black child cannot repeat sentences with any degree of complexity; he tends to "give merely an approximate rendition of the overall sound profile of the sentence."

3. The "culturally deprived" child cannot distinguish sentences that differ with respect to structure words or inflections.

4. "Many disadvantaged children of preschool age come very close to the total lack of ability to use language as a device for acquiring and processing information."

It is true that Bereiter and Engelmann acknowledge that "studies by Loban and others have been cited as evidence that culturally deprived children do possess all the necessary elements of English grammar and syntax, even though they make scanty use of some of them." But, they continue, "what is crucial . . . is not the extent to which their language is technically capable of conveying thoughts and information but the extent to which the children themselves are able to use language in this way."

It is worthy to note that Bereiter and Engelmann apply Bernstein's notion of a "restricted" code to the language of lower-class black children who speak a form of English that is a distinct, nonstandard dialect. While there are dialect differences in England between middle-class and lower-class speech, Bernstein was thinking not so much of dialect differences as of differences in speech styles and modes of formulating thought. Thus, it is easy to gain the false impression, from Bereiter and Engelmann's statements, that lower-class black English is what Bernstein would call a "restricted" code, whereas standard English is an "elaborated" code. The fact of the matter is that if there is any validity in Bernstein's distinction between "restricted" and "elaborated" codes, it could operate just as well in standard English as in some nonstandard form of English such as what is loosely called "lower-class black English." We all use a "restricted" code when we are in casual social situations in which there is quick interchange of simple information, feelings, and opinions that we do not have to formulate carefully.

I have quoted extensively from Bereiter and Engelmann only because they give the most explicit statement available of a view that seems to be widespread: that lower-class black English is "a basically nonlogical mode of expressive behavior which lacks the formal properties necessary for the organization of thought" (Bereiter, et al., 1966, pp. 112–13). It may be that Bereiter and Engelmann no longer hold to this view, but the impression that it has made is sufficiently common among educators to deserve comment and rebuttal. Also, this view reflects social attitudes toward nonstandard languages that linguists feel are misguided and wrong. There are, in fact, many myths about language that are commonly believed and repeated: that simple folk have exceedingly small vocabularies, that the languages of "primitive" tribes are extremely simple and incapable of expressing thought, and that when a person does not speak "grammatically," he is not thinking correctly. The widespread acceptance of such ideas is alarming to linguists, not only because they are scientifically untenable but also because they reflect social attitudes that are rightly to be regarded as snobbish, undemocratic, and antithetical to social progress.

It was for this reason that the Linguistic Society of America last year appointed a Committee on Language and Cognitive Development, of which I am chairman, to prepare materials that would seek to inform educators and the public at large concerning linguists' knowledge about the nature of language, the adequacy of different languages or forms of language for formulating thought, and the nature of language development in the individual. The present address is a brief summary of some of the facts, principles, and views that linguists hope to have made more widely known. These include not only things that linguists as linguists know but also some facts and conclusions that have been reached in the psychology of language.

Let me lay down some general principles that will guide our later consideration of the particular problems of nonstandard dialects:

1. Language is a complex human phenomenon that takes the same general form wherever it is found. It permits the expression of a certain very wide range of information, experiences, feelings, and thoughts, and it does so in somewhat the same way regardless of the particular form of the language or the culture of the user, as long as the language is a so-called "natural language" that is used from childhood on as a native language by its users. This is true whether the language is one such as English, Russian, Chinese, or Indonesian used by a highly developed culture, or one such as Bantu, Navaho, or Fijian, used by a less technically advanced culture. (There are, of course, certain modes of expression, such as music or higher mathematics, that are outside the province of language, but they are equally excluded from all natural languages.)

2. In saying that all languages have the same general form, we mean that all languages possess units for expressing particular concepts and rules whereby utterances are constructed to indicate the social purpose of the utterance and the particular relationships among concepts that are to be communicated. Languages do, of course, differ somewhat in the concepts they select for use in expression, and they vary widely in the particular rules they employ for constructing utterances. Nevertheless, all languages have ways of referring to all the kinds of beings, objects, substances, events, and relationships encountered in common human experience. They all have ways of communicating ideas of space, time, number, negation, condition, opposition, specificity, class membership, quality, and the like, many of these ideas

being of a highly abstract nature. In general, it is true that anything that can be said in one language can be said in any other
language, if one ignores the special connotations and conceptual
references that may attach to the utterances of a given language,
and if one excludes the problem of translating advanced technical ideas from one language to another.

3. Language systems are neutral with respect to truth or logic;
a language system does not force its speakers to make true or
logical statements as opposed to untrue or illogical statements.

4. Except for languages with very small numbers of speakers
living in close association, it is common to find minor or even
major variations in the pronunciation, vocabulary, or grammar of
a language across the various groups using it. Different forms of
a language are technically known as dialects, and to say that a
person speaks a dialect has no derogatory or pejorative force.
Dialect variation occurs both in the languages of advanced civil-
ization (witness all the dialects of English) and in those of
aboriginal groups. It is often the case, too, that one or more
dialects of a language acquire higher status than others; high-
status dialects are generally called standard dialects, while dialects of lesser status are often regarded as nonstandard. This is
not at all because a high-status form of a language is necessarily
any better equipped to communicate ideas or formulate thoughts,
but simply because the speakers of that dialect have attained
generally higher social status and power (and often more education) than the speakers of other dialects through the operation of
political, economic, and other social forces. The phenomenon of
standard vs. nonstandard dialects is found throughout the world,
even in the case of aboriginal languages like Bantu or Fijian, and
speakers of nonstandard dialects are generally well aware of the
low status accorded their dialects, regardless of their actual
social status.

5. Speakers of any language, or dialect, use that language in
many different styles, depending upon the particular social situation in which they find themselves on a given occasion. These
styles or registers vary in many ways, generally along a dimen-

sion of formality vs. informality. For example, Martin Joos in his essay *The Five Clocks* (1967) distinguishes five styles that speakers and writers of standard English may affect: frozen, formal, consultative, casual, and intimate. But he also notes that styles vary in the dimensions of age, "breadth," and "responsibility" (with some overtones of relations with the standard-nonstandard dimension mentioned above). Speakers of nonstandard dialects are capable of similar variation in styles of speech.

6. It is usually the case that the various dialects of a language, whether standard or nonstandard, are mutually intelligible at least to some extent. The more similar the dialects are in their pronunciation, vocabulary, and grammar, the more they are mutually intelligible. Depending upon the amount of exposure to them, and other factors, speakers can learn to understand a number of different dialects better than would otherwise be normal for them. Some speakers can speak and be understood in two or more dialects, often in different levels or registers of these dialects.

7. Within the speakers of a given dialect there will be certain variations in competence, that is, knowledge of the system of the language and the rules by which the system is put together, so to speak. In the main, this variation occurs in the individual's knowledge of vocabulary. That is, some speakers know more words, and more about the different uses of words, than others. There may be some variation also in competence with respect to grammatical rules and even some variation with respect to basic pronunciation rules. These variations in competence depend to an unknown extent on differences in basic mental capacities, in amount of education, or in amount of exposure to other speakers of the language. Through appropriate education or training, individuals can be helped to reach higher levels of competence, but we do not necessarily know what the best training methods are to achieve this goal, nor do we know how to predict the maximum level of competence that an individual can achieve after such training.

8. In addition, even among speakers who have the same degree of competence (technically defined as above), there will be

variation in what we may call performance characteristics, that is, in verbal fluency and creativeness, in reasoning power, in social perception, and other individual traits that affect the individual's use of language, whether in speaking, understanding, reading, or writing. Of course, the more the individual knows about the language, the more likely it is that he will be able to use it fluently, creatively, and intelligently, but it remains true that skill in language use is not only a matter of language competence but of many other factors in the individual's makeup.

9. The course of a child's acquisition of his native language, whatever that language may be, is normally regular and predictable. While there are individual differences in rate of development that may be associated with some combination of hereditary and environmental factors, every child passes through certain distinct stages of development in his learning of the phonological, lexical, and grammatical characteristics of his language. Furthermore, he learns whatever language or variety of language he is exposed to. (Sometimes he learns several languages, or varieties of language, at the same time.) By the time he is about five, the normal child has learned most of the characteristics of his language that enable him to use it in ordinary communication with peers and with adults, although he will learn much more about his language as he grows older and is exposed to more advanced uses of it.

10. The developmental stages through which a child passes in learning his language are quite possibly correlated with the child's mental development. Frankly, we do not know much, as yet, about this correlation or how it operates. There are those who believe that language development leads and guides mental development, and there are those who believe that, on the contrary, mental development leads language development. There is no *a priori* way of resolving this question, and it is difficult even to interpret the few empirical studies that bear on it. On the basis of several lines of reasoning and the available evidence, I incline to the belief that mental development tends to lead and

proceed in advance of language development—that a given stage of language development cannot be attained until the appropriate mental capacity for that development has matured. I believe also that the adequate development of mental maturity is only a *necessary* condition, not a *sufficient* condition, for language development. Obviously, the child must be exposed to language in situations that are meaningful to him before he can learn it. If this view is correct, the absence of a given phase of language development cannot be taken necessarily as evidence of a deficit in mental maturity; it could equally well be evidence of a deficiency in the environmental conditions in which the child is placed.

Armed with these general propositions and principles, we may now re-examine some of the views that have been put forth by such writers as Bernstein, Bereiter and Engelmann, and others.

To say that there exists a "restricted" code in no sense implies that the basic form of a speaker's language is incapable of allowing him to formulate thought of any degree of logical complexity. If one takes the total range of linguistic devices available to the speaker of any natural language, and in fact usually within the competence of that speaker, one finds that these devices would permit the expression of any thought or relationship that one might desire to express (except, of course, for highly technical discourse for which vocabulary might be lacking). Neither British lower-class English, nor lower-class black English is incapable of expressing complex thought. The linguist William Labov (1970) has given a number of examples of lower-class black English in which quite complex thoughts are expressed, for example, one in which a youngster tells a slightly older black interviewer that there can't be a heaven because it could only have been made by a God, but since nobody really knows what God is like, he doesn't exist and therefore couldn't have made a heaven.

Note, however, that this youngster was speaking in a social situation in which he felt perfectly free to talk. If Bereiter's

slum children appeared to speak in "grunts" or "giant words," it
may have been because they found themselves in a situation
which inhibited their speech in certain ways.

Bernstein's "restricted" code is properly to be interpreted as a
style or mode of speaking in which the speaker finds no need to
formulate thoughts carefully with adequate qualification. It has
little or nothing to do with the basic language system in which
the speech is couched, and it is merely an accident if the particular speech patterns used under such conditions appear to be
less complex on the average.

Bereiter and Engelmann's notion that their slum children speak
in "giant words" and are unable to perceive speech as a sequence
of meaningful sounds is patently wrong, as it violates the second
proposition I have enunciated above—that all languages have a
certain form, with rules for constructing utterances out of basic
elements. No language has any provision for constructing "giant
words" that are not analyzable in terms of simpler elements and
that would convey what might otherwise be conveyed by a sentence. Neither the famous compound words of German nor the
polysynthetic words of a language like Eskimo can be conceived
of as "giant words" constructed out of whole cloth, independent
of other elements in the language. Bereiter and Engelmann's
very examples belie their allegations: The child who said "Uai-
ga-nu-ju" (for "I ain't got no juice") *constructed* his utterance
from basic elements according to a fairly complex set of rules; he
could have said "I ain't got no milk" or "I got some juice" or "If
you don't give me no juice, I ain't got none" or literally hundreds
of other utterances on this general pattern.

Since all languages are neutral with respect to truth or logic, it
cannot be the case that nonstandard forms of English are illogical. Under certain conditions, black English omits the copula
to be, as in the utterance "He sick," a fact from which it is sometimes concluded that black English is "illogical." As it happens,
standard Russian also omits the copula in sentences of this type,
but I hope nobody would argue that Russian is "illogical." The
same goes for the argument that languages that use the double

negative are illogical. Black English is similar to French, Spanish, and Old English in using the double negative.

Lower-class black English is admittedly a nonstandard dialect of English, but I believe the status in which it is regarded, like the status of many other nonstandard dialects, would be improved if the public realized that it is just as highly structured and just as capable of communicating thought as a standard dialect. Even if Bernstein's distinction between "restricted" and "elaborated" codes is accepted, there can be both "restricted" and "elaborated" codes, or modes of speaking, in nonstandard dialects as well as in standard ones.

Also, just as standard dialects can be used in various styles, so also can nonstandard dialects be used in various styles. It is possible to reinterpret Bereiter and Engelmann's reports of the speech of their slum children by saying that these children were speaking in a special style—a style adopted whenever the children found themselves in a minority position.

Children speaking a nonstandard dialect cannot be expected necessarily to comprehend standard English, although the evidence says that they understand standard English better than speakers of standard English understand their dialect. This fact is not adequately taken into account in a variety of psychological tests. For example, children who speak nonstandard dialects get unfairly low scores on certain subtests of the widely used Illinois Test of Psycholinguistic Abilities (Paraskevopoulos and Kirk, 1969) that require the child to follow the grammatical distinctions observed by standard English. It is a grave mistake, often made, to interpret these low scores as indicating a retarded state of language development, or worse still, a retarded state of mental development. The manual of the ITPA fails to recognize this problem or to warn against such misinterpretations. A fairer test would be one that is designed in terms of the nonstandard dialect in question.

There may be some justice in the claims of Bereiter and Engelmann, and others who have prepared programs of language improvement for speakers of nonstandard English, that some of these children have not learned the words for certain concepts, even in their own dialects, because one can expect differences in the extent to which children have learned such words. The mistake that is often made, however, is to assume that the nonstandard dialect in question lacks these words or has no way of expressing these concepts. Programs of language "improvement," i.e., programs in which children are taught the standard dialect, should be based on careful analyses of what stock of words and concepts is possessed by the nonstandard dialect. It will frequently turn out that a child who seems not to possess a particular feature of a standard dialect already knows a corresponding feature in his nonstandard dialect.

From the proposition that language acquisition is a natural and regular course of development, we can draw the inference that the child who learns a nonstandard dialect learns it in much the same way as do children who acquire standard dialects. If the child's acquisition of a nonstandard dialect is viewed in its own terms rather than in terms of the extent to which he acquires the standard dialect, it will not appear as distorted and unusual as it is often thought to be.

To sum up the argument of this paper, I would emphasize the incorrectness and fallaciousness of the apparently widespread belief that speaking a nonstandard dialect is somehow a sign of a deficiency in thought or in mental development. There may be some connection between language and thought, but it is not exhibited in nonstandard speech. Our children who are speakers of nonstandard dialects—whether they be blacks, Puerto Ricans, or Chicanos, are not the victims of undeveloped language codes. Their languages have principles and rules similar to those that govern any language.

References

Bereiter, Carl, and Engelmann, Siegfried. *Teaching Disadvantaged Children in the Pre-School.* (Englewood Cliffs, N.J.: Prentice-Hall, 1966.)

Bereiter, Carl, et al. "An Academically Oriented Pre-School," *Pre-School Education Today*, Fred M. Hechinger, Ed., 105-35. (New York: Doubleday, 1966.)

Bernstein, Basil. "Linguistic Codes, Hesitation Phenomena, and Intelligence," *Language and Speech*, 5 (January 1962), 31-46.

Bernstein, Basil. "Some Sociological Determinants of Perception: An Inquiry into Sub-Cultural Differences," *British Journal of Sociology*, 9 (June 1958), 159-74.

Joos, Martin. *The Five Clocks*. (New York: Harcourt Brace Jovanovich, 1967.)

Labov, William. "The Logic of Non-Standard English," *Language and Poverty: Perspectives on a Theme*, Frederick Williams, Ed., 153-89. (Chicago: Markham Publishing Company, 1970.)

Lawton, Denis. *Social Class, Language, and Education.* (New York: Schocken Books, 1968.)

Paraskevopoulos, John N., and Kirk, Samuel A. *The Development and Psychometric Characteristics of the Revised Illinois Test of Psycholinguistic Abilities.* (Urbana: University of Illinois Press, 1969.)